# BIG NIGHT IN

# BIG NIGHT IN

DELICIOUS THEMED MENUS TO COOK & EAT AT HOME

RYLAND PETERS & SMALL
LONDON • NEW YORK

*For Auntie Barbie. I hope you and the girls enjoy many fun Big Nights In together!*

**Writer** Katherine Bebo
**Editor** Sarah Vaughan
**Picture researcher** Christina Borsi
**Production controller** Mai-ling Collyer
**Art director** Leslie Harrington
**Editorial director** Julia Charles
**Publisher** Cindy Richards

**Indexer** Vanessa Bird

First published in 2020 by
Ryland Peters & Small
20–21 Jockey's Fields, London WC1R 4BW
and 341 E 116th St, New York NY 10029
www.rylandpeters.com

10 9 8 7 6 5 4 3 2 1

Recipe collection compiled by Sarah Vaughan. Text copyright © Valerie Aikman-Smith, Brontë Aurell, Miranda Ballard, Ghillie Basan, Julz Beresford, Jordan Bourke, Julia Charles, Lydia Clark, Jesse Estes, Ursula Ferrigno, Tori Finch, Ben Fordham & Felipe Fuentes Cruz, Liz Franklin, Acland Geddes, Laura Gladwin, Victoria Glass, Carole Hilker, Jackie Kearney, Jenny Linford, Loretta Liu,

Hannah Miles, Miisa Mink, Nitisha Patel, Louise Pickford, Ben Reed, Annie Rigg, Shelagh Ryan, Thalassa Skinner, Milli Taylor, Leah Vanderveldt, Laura Washburn Hutton. All other text by Katherine Bebo copyright © Ryland Peters & Small 2020.
Design and commissioned photography copyright © Ryland Peters & Small 2020 (see page 176 for a full list of credits).

ISBN: 978-1-78879-192-2

Printed in China

**NOTES**
• Both British (Metric) and American (Imperial plus US cups) measurements are included in these recipes for your convenience. However, it is important to work with one set of measurements only and not alternate between the two within a recipe.
• Ovens should be preheated to the specified temperatures. We recommend using an oven thermometer. If using a fan-assisted oven, adjust temperatures according to the manufacturer's instructions.
• All eggs are medium (UK) or large (US), unless specified as large, in which case US extra-large should be used. Uncooked or partially cooked eggs should not be served to the elderly, young children, pregnant women or those with compromised immune systems.
• When a recipe calls for grated zest of citrus fruit, buy unwaxed fruit and wash well before using. If you can only find treated fruit, scrub to clean well in warm, soapy water before using.

# CONTENTS

Introduction                                          6
Top Tips for a Big Night In                           8

Mexican Fiesta                                        12
Curry & a Beer Night With Friends                     22
Italian Spritz & Pizza Party                          32
Chinese New Year Festivity                            40
Spanish Tapas & Sangria Tasting                       50
Moreish Mezze                                         58
Scandi Fish Affair                                    66
Meat Feast                                            74
Cheese & Chutney Night                                82
Avocadelicious                                        90
Vegan Celebration                                     98
Family Cook-In                                        106
A Night In at the Movies                              114
Bring-the-Party-Home Kebabs & Shots                   122
Super Bowl Chicken Wings Festival                     130
No Messing Board Games Night                          140
Valentine's Dinner Date                               148
Cosy Comfort Food                                     156
Indoor Picnic                                         164

Index                                                 174
Credits                                               176

# INTRODUCTION

Shun the 'out out' crowd and embrace the fact that staying 'in in' is not only a lot cheaper, it's also a lot more fun. Staying in doesn't always have to involve Netflix and your cosiest onesie. It can often mean putting on your glad rags, cooking up a storm and having the time of your life with your nearest and dearest. Your heart will jump with excitement as you hear the doorbell ring with each new guest arriving with a smile, a hug and a bottle.

When you host a Big Night In, you're in the driver's seat; you're not at the whim of arrogant wait staff, erratic bus schedules or Mother Nature, who saw that you'd blow-dried your hair and thought she'd have a giggle with some drizzle at your expense. No, you're in charge! You get to choose the food, the drinks, the music, the decorations... the *je ne sais quoi*. Most importantly, you get to choose your guests – you can decide on a small, intimate affair (the Valentine's Dinner Date chapter would be perfect here) or a larger, more raucous get-together with a gaggle of friends (a No Messing Board Games Night, perhaps?).

Each of the themed chapters in this book lends itself to a Big Night In of fun, laughter and fabulous food. You can transport your guests to Mexico with a spread of burritos, tacos and tequila cocktails to knock their sombreros off; Italy with pizzas, bruschetta and an array of aperitivos; Spain with tremendous tapas, chomp-a-licious churros and straight-up sangria; or China with dreamy dumplings, tempting tofu noodle salad and a year-round Chinese New Year vibe.

Or, if a 'staycation' is more your scene, why not host a Cheese & Chutney Night, A Night In at the Movies or a Family Cook-In? All tastes, flavour combos and oomph aspects have been considered on the following pages. Whether your dining companions are vegans looking for a va-va-voom meal, carnivores craving a meat fix or avocadarians addicted to the green superfood, they won't be disappointed with the fare you serve and the drinks you pour.

You don't have to host a full-on dinner party with place settings, napkin rings and an elaborate centrepiece (although, if the mood takes you, you can if you so desire). The focus here is fun. Fun with friends, fun with family, fun with housemates, fun with your sweetheart, fun with new acquaintances... On your Big Night In, Fun and Food will go hand in hand – and they'll both have a capital F.

So, flick through this book to get your culinary creative juices flowing. Will you be drawn to the chickpea masala, the Greek rice-stuffed tomatoes, the fig and honey ricotta cheesecake or the avocado margarita? Whatever you choose, embrace your theme with aplomb (no, not a plum!) and you'll soon be slicing, simmering, steaming and sautéing your way to earning the accolade of Hostess with the Mostest, or Host with the Most. Because staying in is the new going out.

Wait, is that the doorbell? Ding dong!

# TOP TIPS FOR A BIG NIGHT IN

**IT'S ALL IN THE PLANNING**

When preparing for an evening of entertaining guests with food and drinks, it's much easier for you, the host, to know you've done as much planning and preparation as possible before the 'event' – when your friends or family arrive, you then won't have to spend all of your time in the kitchen, away from the action! Follow these very simple tips for getting ahead before the date.

**Get the date in the diary.** Everyone has such busy lives, so this can often be the hardest part of the planning!

**Know your crowd.** Who are you inviting and what style of food do they like? Are there any dietary requirements or vegetarians? Any menu should suit your guests and the night in you're planning, to have all bases covered. Most recipes in this book have been written for four to six people, but can easily be upped for a larger crowd, or halved for an intimate dinner for two.

**Plan the menu and what you will be drinking.** This is the fun part. Either follow each themed menu fully, mix and match from each or add your own touch. All is perfectly acceptable. It is about sharing time and food with your loved ones and bringing people together.

**Make a shopping list.** As well as stocking your fridge with all the ingredients, this can also include simple decorations and/or flowers, platters and serving pieces – and this need not break the bank. Many superstores now stock beautiful collections of dinnerware that you'll be proud to display all your tasty food on.

**It is okay to cheat a little.** In addition to the delicious dishes in each menu, there is no harm in buying other ready-made sides or nibbles to make it easier for you. A mix of homemade and bought offers a nice balance.

**Feeding a large crowd.** No need to get in a flap, as you have prepared for this. All the menus in this book have some dishes or elements of the recipes that can be prepared in advance. As the host, you want to be all about relaxed entertaining. Choose a selection of dishes that can be made in advance, with fresh or warm additions on the day. And, when a lot of hot dishes are being prepared, stagger their cooking times – where possible – and try not to overcrowd your oven, as this changes cooking temperature and times.

**Plan a cooking schedule.** Work out what can be made ahead and frozen, what can be cooked the day before or on the day, and what can be bought prepared and ready to serve.

**Opt for a 'buffet'.** With this style of entertaining, some of the work is done in advance, which allows you to spend time with your guests. The benefit for guests is they can choose what they would like to eat and in what combination. There are some suggestions for drinks, but the choice is really up to you – why not serve some of your guests' favourite drinks to keep them entertained while you're finishing the food?

**Make enough.** When making some dishes, make extra so that you can serve second helpings. While there is sometimes a bit of extra work in doubling or tripling a recipe, it's rarely double or triple the effort. Plus, you can always enjoy any leftovers!

**Keep it separate.** It's best to store all components separately. Slow-cooked items can then be reheated gently, and if serving with vegetables, they stay fresh and crisp. Having stackable plastic or glass containers helps with storage, and when strapped for capacity, freezer bags save space.

**Enliven with fresh ingredients on the day.** Whether it is green herbs, a crisp salad, toasted nuts, shaved cheese or bright vegetables – a pre-made dish can be enlivened with a suitable garnish or fresh addition. Not only is it aesthetically appealing but it's great for texture and nutritional value.

**Consider any potential entertainment.** That need not mean hiring a performer or purchasing unnecessary equipment, but pre-selecting music or games that all can share can be a fun addition to any gathering. Each menu in this book lends itself to a certain type of theme, so why not embrace it fully and pick your music or games to match?

**Get help with cleaning and other small tasks before and after the party.** Tidying up is the less fun part of the evening, and being responsible for every aspect of the party isn't always practical as 'host', so don't be afraid to delegate small jobs to loved ones. Why not ask one friend to offer round the canapés, another to make sure no-one's glass is empty, enlist some help to collect up dirty dishes and, for someone who knows how to set the party mood, charge them with the task of party playlist organizer.

## THE ELEMENTS OF A PERFECT PARTY

### Setting the table and how to keep things fresh
• Just to make life easier for you, set the table before your guests arrive, whether it's for a help-yourself buffet or a more formal setting. That includes glasses, napkins, salt and pepper and serving ware.
• For fresh ingredients such as salads, crudités and fruit, it is best to prep beforehand and store separately wrapped in clingfilm/plastic wrap or in airtight containers in the fridge. To maximize freshness, replenish in batches – there's no need to bring all the food out at once.
• The same goes for breads and dips – put out half and then top up. Nothing is worse than dried-out bread or crusty dips. Also, it's good to keep back some food just in case some of your guests are running late.
• When serving food at room temperature remember it should be kept like this for a maximum of 2 hours.

### Creating a balance of different foods
• The key to all these menus is the balance between different types of foods such as raw/cooked, hot/cold. Even if a menu is based around one main ingredient or foodie theme, it is this balance that will create an interesting meal and keep you, the host, relaxed.
• Whether it's a starter/appetizer, main or dessert, in most cases it is good to introduce different elements.
• If vegetables are served raw, keep crisp and fresh and, unless pre-washed, wash and thoroughly dry them.
• For anything cooked, again serve in batches – in fact, it's more economical this way. If it's not all eaten, then you can reserve the rest for supper or work lunches.
• For warmed food, some dishes are delicious warm but can also be eaten at room temperature. It is with these dishes that you can serve fresh, crisp raw sides.

### Decorating and making your tables and platters fun
• Decorations need not be extravagant; a hint of glam and elegance is great, but not if it breaks the bank. Some carefully positioned candles, attractively folded napkins or handwritten namecards or menus will add just the *oomph* the table might need.
• The best decoration is the best-quality ingredients you can find. Use them in an eye-catching salad, serve them as crudités or have a bowl of gorgeous vegetables or fruit to nibble on – nothing is more beautiful.
• To keep the gathering and the table relaxed, don't be tempted to overwhelm your guests with too much at the table. A pretty vase of flowers, a bowl of beautiful lemons, pots of fresh herbs or a few lovely succulents add an understated yet decorative touch.
• Let the food celebrate itself. A table that has mixed fruit with vegetables, jugs/pitchers of drinks, breads, nibbles, flowers, ambient food on platters and warmed food on boards, plus the company of your friends and family, will make a perfect gathering.

## FREEZER AND STORE CUPBOARD/PANTRY ESSENTIALS

The items below form a great list of what you might want to keep in your freezer, fridge and cupboard/pantry. Many essentials are included in this book – from seasonings and garnishes, to party nibbles – and are handy 'go-tos' for livening up an everyday dish.

### FREEZER

- Soups
- Pre-made casseroles
- Pizza dough, after its first rise
- Ice – ALWAYS
- Frozen berries
- Smoothie mixes
- Frozen prawns/shrimp
- Good-quality stock
- Flavoured butters
- Broad/fava beans
- Peas

### STORE CUPBOARD/PANTRY

- Sea salt flakes
- Ground black pepper (or peppercorns in a grinder)
- Extra virgin olive oil
- Flavourless oils for baking and frying
- Flavoured oils for dressings, such as walnut, sesame or chilli/chili
- Vinegars: balsamic, red-wine, apple cider, sherry
- Spices and dried herbs
- Dried chilli/hot red pepper flakes
- Soy sauce
- Miso
- Dijon mustard
- Wholegrain mustard
- Capers
- Worcestershire sauce

- Sriracha or other hot sauce
- Honey
- Canned beans
- Grains
- Rice
- Tortilla chips and/or breadsticks
- Passata/tomato pureé and/or sun-dried tomato paste
- Kalamata olives, green olives
- Artichoke hearts
- All sorts of nuts
- All sorts of seeds
- Chocolate
- Green tea
- Wine, beer or spirits of choice (including any mixers)

### FRIDGE AND FRESH

- Citrus: oranges, lemons, grapefruit, limes
- Onions, white and red
- Potatoes
- Leafy greens
- Garlic
- Spring onions/scallions
- Tomatoes
- Fresh herbs
- Parmesan cheese and/or vegetarian option
- Feta cheese
- Greek yogurt
- Hummus (or other popular dips)
- Eggs

# MEXICAN FIESTA

Whether served at home or during one of the many famous festivals, food is a huge part of the Mexican culture, bringing families, friends and whole communities together. With this unapologetically peppy menu, there's enough fire to keep you and your compadres zinging through the week. Why not roll Margarita Mondays, Taco Tuesdays, Tequila Thursdays and Salsa Saturdays into one night with this 'mazing Mexican meal? Your guests are in for some serious gauc 'n' roll!

## SMALL PLATES & SIDES
Mexican-Style Beans
Guacamole
Roasted Tomato Salsa
Elotes (Grilled Corn)

## BIGGER BITES
Chicken Tinga Tacos
Orange-Braised Pork Burritos

## DRINKS
Classic Margarita
Tequila Beyond Sunrise

# MEXICAN-STYLE BEANS

4 garlic cloves, unpeeled
4 plum tomatoes, chopped
1 chipotle chilli/chile in
   adobo sauce
½ teaspoon ground cumin

2 x 400-g/14-oz. cans black
   or pinto beans, drained
2 tablespoons vegetable oil
fine sea salt

**SERVES 6–8**

Heat a ridged stove-top griddle/grill pan until hot.
Cook the garlic and tomatoes over high heat for
3–5 minutes until charred, then let cool. When cool,
slip the garlic cloves out of their skins. Put the garlic,
tomatoes, chilli/chile, cumin and beans
in a blender and work to a coarse purée.

Heat the oil in a saucepan over medium
heat. Add the bean mixture and cook
for 15–20 minutes, stirring often, until
thick. Taste and adjust the seasoning
with salt. Serve hot.

# GUACAMOLE

2 ripe avocados, peeled,
   stoned/pitted and
   chopped
2–3 tablespoons sour/
   soured cream
juice of ½ lemon

1 small bunch of coriander/
   cilantro, finely chopped
a pinch of ground cumin
½ teaspoon fine sea salt
1 small chilli/chile, green
   or red (optional)

**SERVES 4–6**

Put the avocados in a small bowl and mash
to a coarse paste using a fork.

Stir in the sour/soured cream, lemon juice, coriander/
cilantro, cumin, salt and chilli/chile, if using.

Mix well. Taste and adjust the seasoning, adding
more salt or lemon juice, as desired.

# ROASTED TOMATO SALSA

950 g/2 lbs. 2 oz. ripe
   tomatoes
1 large onion, thickly sliced
4 green chillies/chiles
1 small bunch of fresh
   coriander/cilantro

a pinch of sugar
2 tablespoons lime juice
fine sea salt, to season

**SERVES 4–6**

Heat a ridged stove-top griddle/grill pan over
a high heat. Add the tomatoes, onion and chillies/
chiles and cook for 3–5 minutes on each side until
charred all over.

Put the onion, tomatoes, chillies/chiles and
coriander/cilantro in a blender and work to a coarse
purée. Transfer to a bowl and stir in the sugar, lime
juice and season with salt. Chill until needed, then
serve this and the Guacamole at room temperature.

Note: These three dips make delicious nibbles when
served with oven-warmed corn tortillas, or with the
Baked Tortilla Chips (see page 100).

# CHICKEN TINGA TACOS

500 g/1 lb. 2 oz skinless, boneless
    chicken breasts
1 large onion, chopped
3 tomatoes, cut into wedges
2 garlic cloves, peeled
2 tablespoons chipotle chilli/chili paste
3/4 teaspoon freshly ground white pepper
1 tablespoon paprika
1 1/2 teaspoons salt
2 tablespoons vegetable oil

TO SERVE
12 flour or corn tortillas, warmed
1/2 romaine lettuce, shredded
1 bunch of radishes, sliced
1/2 red onion, sliced
150 ml/2/3 cup sour/soured cream
200 g/7 oz. feta cheese, crumbled

SERVES 3–4

Place the chicken in a small saucepan with 1 litre/quart water and bring to a boil, then simmer for 10 minutes. Skim the froth from the top if necessary. Remove the pan from the heat. Lift the chicken from the pan with a slotted spoon and set aside to cool. Pour the broth into a separate bowl and reserve for later. When the chicken is cool enough to handle, shred into small pieces.

In the now-empty saucepan, place 20 g/2 tablespoons of the onion, the tomatoes and garlic and 500 ml/2 cups water, bring to a boil, then simmer for 5 minutes. Drain, discard the water and let cool. Once cooled, place in a blender with the chipotle paste, white pepper, paprika and salt and blend until smooth.

Take the saucepan again and heat the oil, then add the remaining chopped onion. Sauté for 1 minute, then add the shredded chicken and the mixture from the blender and cook for another minute. Add 125 ml/1/2 cup of the reserved chicken broth and simmer over low heat for 15 minutes.

To serve, place a generous spoonful of chicken tinga on top of each warmed tortilla. Top up with the lettuce, radishes, red onion, sour/soured cream and finally the crumbled feta cheese.

# ELOTES (GRILLED CORN)

vegetable oil, for brushing
1 teaspoon chilli/chili powder
1/2 teaspoon cayenne pepper
8 corn on the cob/ears of corn
60 g/1/4 cup mayonnaise or unsalted butter
65 g/1/2 cup crumbled Cotija, Parmesan
    or ricotta salata cheese
1 lime, cut into 8 wedges

SERVES 8

Preheat a grill/broiler to medium-high and brush the rack with oil. Combine the chilli/chili powder and cayenne in a small bowl.

Grill/broil the corn for about 10 minutes, turning occasionally with tongs, until cooked through and lightly charred. Remove from the grill/broiler and brush each cob/ear with 1 1/2 teaspoons of mayonnaise or butter. Sprinkle each with a tablespoon of cheese and a pinch of the chilli/chili-cayenne mixture. Squeeze a lime wedge over each cob/ear and serve.

Alternatively, remove the corn kernels from the cobs/ears, after taking them off the grill/broiler, and combine the corn with the mayonnaise or butter and the cheese. Top with the chilli/chili-cayenne mixture and a squeeze of lime juice.

# ORANGE-BRAISED PORK BURRITOS

1.2 kg/2 lbs. 10 oz. bonless
    pork, with fat, shoulder
    or leg, cut into chunks
juice of 3–4 oranges
2 garlic cloves, crushed
1 teaspoon fine sea salt
a pinch of ground allspice
1 teaspoon ground cumin
300 g/1½ cups cooked rice
4–6 large flour tortillas
180 g/1²/₃ cups grated/
    shredded cheddar or
    Monterey Jack cheese
vegetable oil, for oiling

freshly ground black
    pepper, to season

**CHILLI/CHILI PURÉE**
3 dried ancho chillies/
    chiles, deseeded
1 onion, coarsely chopped
60 ml/¼ cup apple cider
    vinegar
½ teaspoon dried oregano
½ teaspoon ground cumin
1 teaspoon fine sea salt

**SERVES 4–6**

Preheat the oven to 200°C (400°F) Gas 6.

Combine the pork, orange juice, garlic, salt, allspice and cumin in a large casserole dish. Set over high heat and bring to a boil. Lower the heat and simmer for 1½–2 hours, uncovered, until tender. Let cool, cover and refrigerate until needed.

To prepare the chilli/chile purée, soak the chillies/chiles in boiling water for 15 minutes. Remove the chillies/chiles and reserve the liquid. Remove the stems from the chillies/chiles and put them in a food processor with the onion, vinegar, oregano, cumin, salt and 375 ml/1½ cups of the soaking liquid. Blend until a smooth paste.

Remove the pork from the casserole dish and reserve the cooking liquid. Using your hands, or two forks, separate the meat from the fat and shred the meat. Remove any fat from the surface of the cooking liquid and return it to the casserole dish with the shredded meat. Stir in the rice and chilli/chile purée. Simmer for 10 minutes. Taste and adjust the seasoning.

Divide the pork mixture between the tortillas and sprinkle with the grated/shredded cheese. Fold in the sides of each tortilla to cover the filling, then roll up. Place the filled tortillas seam-side down on an oiled baking sheet or in a shallow dish. Cover with foil and bake in the preheated oven for 10–15 minutes just to warm through and melt the cheese. Serve hot.

Who's for margaritas with your señoritas (and hombres)? While you're chippin' and dippin', do some cocktail sippin'. Ask Alexa to crank up Alan Jackson's 'Mexico, Tequila and Me' as you play bartender to mix your gasping guests these tequila-tastic treats. Encourage them to sip and sing while the country music legend tells them of his plans to 'take a three-day breather, sip a margarita' and 'drift away beside the sea'.

## TEQUILA BEYOND SUNRISE

45 ml/1½ fl. oz. Ocho
   Reposado Tequila
60 ml/2 fl. oz. fresh
   orange juice
15 ml/½ fl. oz. freshly
   squeezed lime juice
10 ml/2 teaspoons simple
   sugar syrup
10 ml/2 teaspoons
   egg white
5 ml/1 teaspoon yuzu juice
a pinch of sea salt

ice cubes
15 ml/½ fl. oz.
   Pomegranate, Port
   and Chipotle Reduction
   (see Note)

TO GARNISH
orange zest
maraschino cherry and a
   cocktail stick/toothpick

MAKES 1

Add all the drink ingredients (except the reduction) to a cocktail shaker with cubed ice. Shake and strain into a highball glass over cubed ice. Add the reduction over the top of the drink, to give the 'sunrise' look. Carefully peel a long strip of orange zest to garnish with an orange zest and cherry 'flag', as pictured.

Note: To make the Pomegranate, Port & Chipotle Reduction, add 500 ml/2 cups freshly squeezed pomegranate juice and 500 ml/2 cups ruby port to a saucepan and simmer for about 45 minutes until reduced by half. Next, add 500 g/2½ cups light brown muscovado/packed light brown sugar and 2 teaspoons chipotle chilli/chili powder and stir until dissolved. Store in a sealed bottle in the fridge for up to 2 weeks.

## CLASSIC MARGARITA

lime wedge and sea salt
   flakes, for the glass rim
50 ml/1²/₃ fl. oz. Ocho
   Blanco Tequila
25 ml/³/₄ fl. oz. freshly

squeezed lime juice
25 ml/³/₄ fl. oz. Cointreau
ice cubes

MAKES 1

Rub the outer rim of a chilled margarita glass with the lime wedge. Dip the glass rim into the sea salt flakes, so that the salt remains on the outside of the glass. Add the rest of the drink ingredients to a cocktail shaker with cubed ice and shake hard. Double strain into the salt-rimmed margarita glass.

# CURRY & A BEER NIGHT WITH FRIENDS

Calling all spice girls (and boys). Transform your dining room into
a comforting curry house complete with free-flowing beer and second-
to-naan banter. To liven up the atmosphere even more, why not use
a long strip of bright Indian fabric as a tablecloth or table runner?
Try not to freak out when your guests inevitably spill globs of masala
on it, though – just keep calm and curry on.

## SMALL PLATES & SIDES

Samosas

Coconut Rice

Potato Pakoras

Naani Maa's Lemon Pickle

Tomato, Cucumber & Mint Raita

## BIGGER BITES

Chickpea Masala

Gosht Aloo Saag Masala

# SAMOSAS

**SAMOSA FILLING**
60 ml/¹⁄₄ cup vegetable oil
1 teaspoon cumin seeds
1¹⁄₂ teaspoons coriander seeds, crushed
¹⁄₂ teaspoon finely chopped green
    chilli/chile
1 teaspoon grated fresh root ginger
350 g/12 oz. boiled, crushed potatoes
    (Maris Piper or Yukon Gold, boiled
    and broken with hands; not mashed)
1 teaspoon salt
¹⁄₂ teaspoon chilli/chili powder
75 g/1 cup frozen peas, thawed
1 tablespoon chopped coriander/cilantro
vegetable oil, for deep-frying

**PASTRY**
200 g/1²⁄₃ cups plain/all-purpose flour
¹⁄₂ teaspoon ajwain seeds
¹⁄₂ teaspoon salt
2 tablespoons melted ghee
60 ml/¹⁄₄ cup hot water (not boiling)

**MAKES 16**

Start by making the samosa filling. Heat the vegetable oil in a pan over medium heat. Add the cumin seeds and fry until they start to sizzle, then add the crushed coriander seeds and fry for 15 seconds. Add the green chilli/chile and ginger and fry for about 20 seconds. Add the crushed potatoes, salt and chilli/chili powder and stir well in the oil until all of the potato is coated. Cook until the potatoes are warmed through, then add the peas and chopped coriander/cilantro and mix well. Transfer the filling to a baking sheet or large plate, spread out and let cool.

To make the pastry, put the flour, ajwain seeds and salt in a bowl and mix. Pour in the melted ghee and gently rub in using your fingertips. When the ghee is well distributed in the flour, pour in the hot water, a little at a time, and bring the mixture together to form a dough. Knead and work the dough until it is smooth with no visible cracks – it should be the same texture as bread dough. Cover the dough with some greased clingfilm/plastic wrap and set aside.

Once the filling has cooled completely, make the pastry sheets for each individual samosa. Divide the dough into eight even balls and roll out to 12.5-cm/5-inch circles. Cut each circle in half, creating 16 equal semicircles.

Build the samosas one by one by making a cone shape with a semicircle of pastry; bring one side to overlap with the other side of the pastry and seal the edge together with a little water. Gently hold the cone in one hand (do not allow the cone to close while it is empty, as the pastry may stick together) and pinch the tip to seal. Using a teaspoon, spoon a little of the filling into the pastry cone, then use the spoon as an aid to gently push in the filling. Do not overfill; leave a lip of pastry (around 1 cm/¹⁄₂ inch). Using your fingertips, brush a little water around the inner exposed part of the pastry and seal by pressing the two sides together to form a sealed triangle. Repeat to create 16 samosas.

Heat the oil for deep-frying in a deep-fat fryer or large, heavy-bottomed pan to 180°C (350°F). Deep-fry the samosas, in batches of 4–5, until golden brown; this should take 5–6 minutes.

Drain on paper towels and set aside until ready to serve.

# COCONUT RICE

225 g/1¼ cups basmati rice
2 tablespoons sunflower oil
2 teaspoons black mustard seeds
2 teaspoons cumin seeds
2 dried red chillies/chiles
10 fresh curry leaves
500 ml/2 cups hot water
60 ml/¼ cup coconut cream
2 tablespoons freshly grated/shredded
   fresh coconut, to garnish

**Serves 4**

Rinse the rice until the water runs clear. Transfer to a bowl, cover with cold water and let soak for 15 minutes. Drain thoroughly.

Heat the sunflower oil in a heavy-bottomed saucepan and add the mustard seeds, cumin seeds, chillies/chiles and curry leaves. Stir-fry for 30 seconds, then add the hot water and coconut cream. Stir well and bring to a boil. Reduce the heat to low, cover tightly and cook for 10 minutes.

Let stand undisturbed for 10 minutes. Fluff up the rice with a fork and scatter over the grated/shredded coconut.

Fries, mashed, baked, roasted, boiled, dauphinoise, gnocchi... The humble potato wears many hats (and jackets). Whip up this recipe – combining herbs, spices and more than a dash of delicious – for your Indian-inspired evening and say 'later tater' to simple spuds.

# POTATO PAKORAS

190 g/2 cups chickpea/gram flour
1½ teaspoons salt, plus extra for seasoning
1 teaspoon garam masala
½ teaspoon chilli/chili powder
½ teaspoon ground turmeric
1 teaspoon nigella seeds (kalonji)
300 g/10½ oz. potatoes
1 large onion, finely chopped
1 garlic clove, finely chopped
1 small bunch of coriander/cilantro, finely
    chopped, plus extra leaves to garnish
juice of ½ lime
150 ml/²/3 cup natural/plain yogurt
vegetable or sunflower oil, for deep-frying

**MAKES ABOUT 32**

First make the batter. Sift the chickpea/gram flour, 1½ teaspoons salt, the garam masala, chilli/chili powder and turmeric into a mixing bowl. Beat in 200 ml/³/4 cup water to form a thick batter. Stir in the nigella seeds and set aside to rest for 30 minutes.

Peel and finely dice the potatoes. Mix the potatoes, onion, garlic and 4 tablespoons/¼ cup of the chopped coriander/cilantro into the batter.

Make a dipping sauce by mixing the remaining coriander/cilantro and lime juice into the yogurt. Season with salt. Set aside.

Heat enough oil for deep-frying in a deep pan or wok to 180°C (350°F) or until a small piece of bread added to the hot oil browns within 60 seconds.

Fry the pakoras in batches. To form the individual pakoras, drop spoonfuls of the potato mixture, spaced apart, into the hot oil. Fry until they turn a rich golden brown on all sides. Remove with a slotted spoon, drain on paper towels and keep warm.

Once all the batter has been used up, serve the pakoras at once accompanied by the yogurt dipping sauce and garnished with coriander/cilantro leaves.

# CHICKPEA MASALA

60 ml/¼ cup sunflower oil
4 garlic cloves, crushed
2 teaspoons finely grated
  fresh root ginger
1 large onion, coarsely
  grated
1–2 green chillies/chiles,
  thinly sliced
1 teaspoon hot chilli
  powder, plus extra
  to garnish
1 tablespoon ground cumin
1 tablespoon ground
  coriander

3 tablespoons plain/natural
  yogurt, plus extra,
  whipped, to drizzle
2 teaspoons garam masala
2 teaspoons tamarind paste
2 teaspoons medium curry
  powder
2 x 400-g/14-oz. cans
  chickpeas, drained
  and rinsed
chopped coriander/cilantro
  leaves, to garnish
lemon wedges, to serve
  (optional)

**SERVES 4**

Heat the sunflower oil in a large, heavy-bottomed frying pan/skillet over medium heat and add the garlic, ginger, onion and chillies/chiles. Stir-fry for 6–8 minutes, or until lightly golden. Add the chilli/chili powder, cumin, ground coriander, plain/natural yogurt and garam masala and stir-fry for 1–2 minutes.

Stir in 500 ml/2 cups water and bring to a boil. Add the tamarind paste, curry powder and chickpeas and bring back to a boil. Reduce the heat to low and simmer for 30–40 minutes, stirring occasionally, or until the liquid has reduced, coating the chickpeas in a dark, rich sauce.

Serve in bowls drizzled with a little whipped yogurt, garnished with chopped coriander/cilantro and chilli/chili powder, and with lemon wedges on the side, if liked.

# GOSHT ALOO SAAG MASALA

1 kg/2¼ lbs. leg of lamb
    on the bone, portioned
    into pieces
rice or naan bread, to serve

### HOLY TRINITY PASTE
200 g/7 oz. (about 60)
    green chillies/chiles
200 g/7 oz. (about 40)
    garlic cloves, peeled
200 g/7 oz. (about 8 x
    5-cm/2-inch pieces)
    fresh root ginger
50 ml/3½ tablespoons
    vegetable oil
1 tablespoon salt

### MARINADE
5 tablespoons vegetable oil
2 teaspoons salt
2 teaspoons Holy Trinity
    Paste (see above)
1 teaspoon ground turmeric
1 teaspoon ground cumin
1 teaspoon ground
    coriander
1 teaspoon chilli/chili
    powder
1 teaspoon garam masala
2 tablespoons natural/
    plain yogurt
1 teaspoon chickpea/gram
    flour

### CURRY SAUCE
6 tablespoons vegetable oil
a 1.5-cm/5/8-inch piece
    of cassia bark
2 star anise
6 cloves
6 cardamom pods
1 teaspoon cumin seeds
1 tablespoon fine julienne
    of fresh root ginger
3 garlic cloves, thinly sliced
2 large onions, finely
    chopped
1 teaspoon salt
3 tablespoons tomato
    purée/paste
1 large tomato, chopped
    (core and seeds removed)
5 potatoes (Maris Piper
    or Yukon Gold, about
    430 g/15 oz. in total),
    peeled and quartered
1 teaspoon garam masala
1 tablespoon chopped
    coriander/cilantro
1 tablespoon chopped mint
juice of ½ lemon

### SPINACH PURÉE
400 g/14 oz. baby spinach
    leaves
1 tablespoon melted ghee

**SERVES 6**

First, make the Holy Trinity Paste. Blitz together the ingredients in a food processor until coarse. Refrigerate in an airtight container for up to 2 weeks.

Combine all of the ingredients for the marinade in a large mixing bowl, add the lamb and stir to coat. Set aside at room temperature for 30 minutes, then refrigerate for a minimum of 24 hours.

To make the curry sauce, heat the oil in a heavy-bottomed pan over medium heat. Add the cassia bark, star anise, cloves and cardamom pods and fry for 1 minute to release the natural oils, then add the cumin seeds and fry for an additional 1 minute.

Add the ginger and garlic and fry until light brown. Add the onions and salt and fry gently until softened and golden brown. (This may take 25–30 minutes, but be patient and let the onions fry slowly.)

Add the marinated lamb, mix well and cook for 30 minutes, stirring occasionally, to seal the meat.

Add the tomato purée/paste, stir in and let simmer for 3 minutes. Add the tomato and cook for 15 minutes or until the tomato completely melts into the sauce. Once the sauce has become nice and rich, add 1 litre/quart water and the potatoes. Cover with a lid, reduce the heat and simmer for 30 minutes until the potatoes are cooked.

To make the spinach purée, put the baby spinach into a food processor and pour in the melted ghee. Blitz the spinach and ghee together until the mixture forms a purée. Set aside.

Add the garam masala, coriander/cilantro, mint, spinach purée and lemon juice to the sauce and mix well. Remove from the heat and serve with rice or naan bread.

# NAANI MAA'S LEMON PICKLE

500 g/1 lb. 2 oz. lemons
4 teaspoons rock salt
1 teaspoon ground turmeric
2 teaspoons chilli/chili powder
1 teaspoon ground coriander
1 teaspoon ground cumin
1 teaspoon ground ginger
3 tablespoons vegetable oil
a 5-cm/2-inch cinnamon stick
1 teaspoon cumin seeds
1 teaspoon fennel seeds
500 g/2½ cups palm sugar/jaggery

*a sterilized glass jar fitted with an airtight lid*

**SERVES 16**

Bring a pan of water to a boil. Add the lemons whole and boil them for 8–10 minutes or until soft, then drain. Cut each lemon into eight equal wedges and put them in a large mixing bowl (adding all the excess lemon juice as well). Sprinkle over the salt, turmeric, chilli/chili powder, ground coriander, cumin and ginger. Mix well.

Heat the oil in a heavy-bottomed pan over medium heat, add the cinnamon stick and cumin seeds and let sizzle and crackle. Add the fennel seeds and toss in the hot oil for 20 seconds. Pour this over the lemons and mix well. Set aside.

Add the palm sugar/jaggery and 3 tablespoons water to another pan and mix well. Set over low heat to let the sugar to dissolve into the water slowly.

Once the sugar water has become a syrup, add the lemon wedges and any excess juices that may have been released along with the seasoned oil. Mix well and simmer gently for 2 minutes. Do not let the lemons boil, as the pickle will become bitter.

Store the lemon pickle in the sterilized glass jar fitted with an airtight lid. It should last for up to 3 months at room temperature – once opened, store in the fridge for up to 2 weeks.

# TOMATO, CUCUMBER & MINT RAITA

1 teaspoon cumin seeds
500 ml/2 cups natural/plain yogurt
1 large tomato, finely chopped
   (core and seeds removed)
½ cucumber, grated
6 large mint leaves, finely chopped,
   plus extra to garnish
1 teaspoon salt
1 teaspoon caster/granulated sugar
a pinch of chilli/chili powder

**SERVES 4**

Toast the cumin seeds in a dry frying pan/skillet until they darken and become aromatic with an earthy fragrance. Pound the seeds using a pestle and mortar to form a powder and set aside.

Whip the yogurt in a large mixing bowl until smooth. Add all the remaining ingredients, including the ground cumin, check the seasoning and serve, garnished with mint. Store in the fridge if not required straight away.

# ITALIAN SPRITZ
# &
# PIZZA PARTY

Movie star and self-confessed pizza fan Bill Murray has his priorities
straight, once famously saying, 'Unless you are a pizza, the answer is yes,
I can live without you.' If pizza is the only love triangle you ever want
to be involved in, this menu will shape your dinner party perfectly.
Whichever way you slice it, your guests are in for a real treat of cheesy,
tomatoey deliciousness, topped off with some sparkling splashes
of scrumptious. Mamma mia!

## SMALL PLATES & SIDES

Cherry Tomato Bruschetta
Assorted Focaccia Crostini

## BIGGER BITES

Mushroom & Parma Ham Pizza
Sardinian Pizza

## DRINKS

The Perfect Spritz
Negroni
Tintoretto

# CHERRY TOMATO BRUSCHETTA

1 slender baguette
2 teaspoons olive oil
12 red and yellow cherry tomatoes,
    quartered
1 teaspoon balsamic vinegar
a pinch of salt
1 garlic clove, peeled
4–6 basil leaves, plus extra to garnish
freshly ground black pepper, for sprinkling

**MAKES ABOUT 12**

Preheat the oven to 200°C (400°F) Gas 6. Slice the baguette into 1-cm/½-inch-thick slices. Transfer to a baking sheet and lightly brush with 1 teaspoon of the oil. Bake in the oven for 20 minutes until pale gold and crisp. Remove from the oven and let cool.

Meanwhile, mix together the cherry tomatoes with the remaining olive oil, balsamic vinegar, salt and whole garlic clove in a large bowl. Shred the basil leaves and mix in. Set aside to let the flavours infuse while the baguette slices bake and cool.

Discard the garlic clove from the tomato mixture, then spoon onto each slice of bread. Garnish with basil leaves and sprinkle with pepper. Serve at once.

# MUSHROOM & PARMA HAM PIZZA

500 g/3¾ cups strong white/bread flour,
    plus extra for dusting
1 teaspoon fast-action dried/rapid-rise
    dry yeast
1 teaspoon salt
½ teaspoon sugar
250–275 ml/1–scant 1¼ cups warm water
50 ml/3½ tablespoons olive oil
500 g/1 lb. 2 oz. white mushrooms,
    sliced 5-mm/¼-inch thick
1 garlic clove, chopped
2 balls mozzarella cheese,
    torn into pieces
4 slices Parma ham/prosciutto,
    roughly torn
chopped parsley, to garnish
2 tablespoons truffle oil (optional)
salt and freshly ground black pepper,
    to season

*pizza stones (optional)*

**MAKES 4**

For the dough, place the flour, yeast, salt and sugar in a large bowl and mix together. Gradually mix in the warm water to form a soft dough. Knead on a floured surface for 10 minutes until supple. Place the dough in a floured bowl and cover with a clean tea/kitchen towel. Set aside in a warm place for 1 hour to rise and double in size.

Preheat the oven to 240°C (475°F) Gas 9. Place the pizza stones, if using, or baking sheets in the oven to preheat.

Heat a large, heavy frying pan/skillet. Add 1 tablespoon of the olive oil, heat, then fry the mushrooms for 8 minutes until they are lightly browned. Add an additional ½ tablespoon olive oil, heat and fry the garlic for 1 minute. Season with salt and pepper. Set aside.

Divide the risen dough into four equal portions. Roll out each on a lightly floured work surface to form an oval pizza base/crust. Brush each base/crust evenly with ½ tablespoon of the olive oil. Sprinkle each equally with the fried mushrooms. Dot with the mozzarella.

Transfer to the hot pizza stones or hot baking sheets, then bake the pizzas, in batches if necessary, in the preheated oven for 10 minutes until the dough is golden brown. Top the pizzas with the Parma ham/prosciutto and sprinkle with parsley. Drizzle ½ tablespoon truffle oil over each pizza, if using. Slice and serve at once.

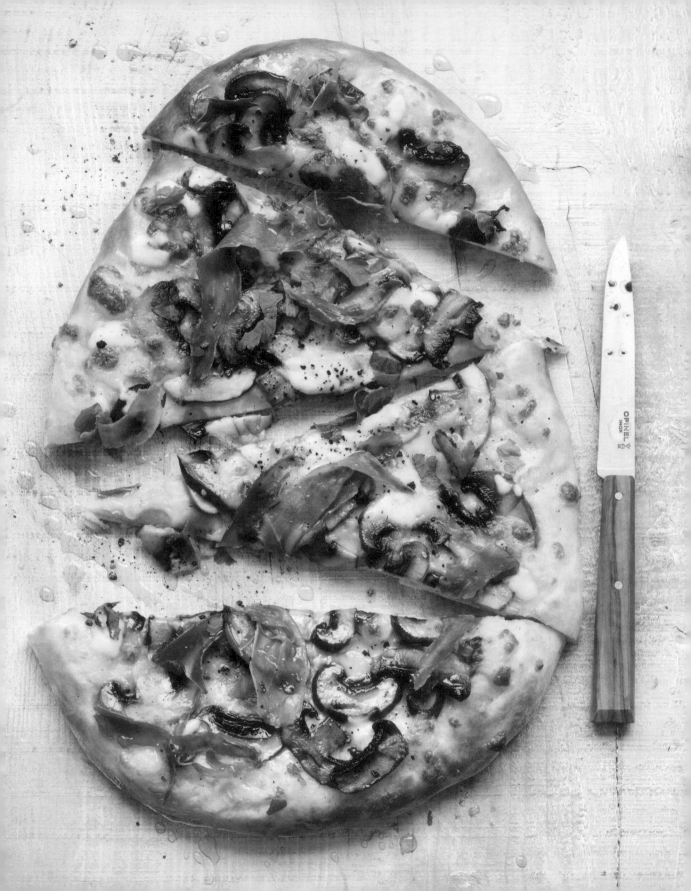

# SARDINIAN PIZZA

**PIZZA DOUGH**
15 g/½ oz. fresh yeast or
    7 g/¼ oz. dried active/
    active dry yeast
4 tablespoons warm water
225 g/1⅔ cups strong
    white/bread flour, plus
    extra for dusting
1 teaspoon fine sea salt
65 g/4½ tablespoons
    unsalted butter
1 UK large/US extra-large
    egg, beaten
olive oil, for oiling

**PIZZA TOPPING**
5 tablespoons olive oil

750 g/1 lb. 10 oz. onions,
    finely sliced
500 g/1 lb. 2 oz. ripe
    tomatoes, skinned
    and roughly chopped
55 g/2 oz. anchovy fillets
a handful of black olives,
    halved and pitted
a handful of oregano
sea salt and freshly ground
    black pepper, to season
chilli/chili oil, to serve

*two 20–23-cm/8–9-inch
    round shallow baking
    pans*

**SERVES 8**

To make the pizza dough, blend the yeast with the water. Mix the flour and salt together in a large bowl. Rub the butter into the seasoned flour with your fingertips, then make a well in the centre. Add the egg and the yeast mixture and mix to a firm but pliable dough. Add more water if necessary. When the dough has come away cleanly from the sides of the bowl, turn out onto a floured work surface and knead thoroughly for 10 minutes. Gather into a ball, place in a clean oiled bowl and cover with clingfilm/plastic wrap and let rise in a warm place until doubled in size, about 1½ hours.

When the dough has risen, turn it out onto a lightly floured work surface, divide into two and knead each piece lightly. Oil the pans well, then place the dough in the pans and press out with floured knuckles. Cover the pans with clingfilm/plastic wrap and preheat the oven to 200°C (400°F) Gas 6 while you prepare the topping.

To make the topping, heat the olive oil in a frying pan/skillet and sauté the onions gently, covered, stirring now and then, until soft, about 20 minutes. Add the tomatoes and salt and pepper and cook, uncovered, until the sauce is thick. Let cool.

When cold, divide the topping between the pizzas, spreading it evenly. Criss-cross the surface with strips of anchovy and put the olive halves in the spaces. Sprinkle with the oregano and bake in the preheated oven for 25 minutes until golden brown and bubbling. Drizzle with chilli/chili oil to serve.

# ASSORTED FOCACCIA CROSTINI

500 g/3¾ cups strong white/bread flour, plus extra for dusting

7-g sachet/package or 2¼ level teaspoons fast-action dried/rapid-rise dry yeast

1 teaspoon fine sea salt

4 tablespoons extra virgin olive oil, plus extra for oiling

300 ml/1¼ cups hand-hot water

2 tablespoons rosemary leaves

2 generous teaspoons sea salt flakes

1 garlic clove, peeled

## GARLIC MUSHROOM TOPPING

1 tablespoon olive oil

15 g/1 tablespoon unsalted butter

1 shallot, finely chopped

250 g/½ lb. mixed wild mushrooms

1 tablespoon chopped flat-leaf parsley

## MEDITERRANEAN TOMATOES TOPPING

4 ripe tomatoes, chopped

1 roasted red (bell) pepper, from a jar, chopped

1 tablespoon basil leaves, torn

1 tablespoon mixed pitted olives, chopped

100 g/3½ oz. buffalo mozzarella, torn

## BEANS & MINT TOPPING

175 g/1¼ cups broad/fava beans and/or peas

1 tablespoon chopped mint

grated zest of ½ lemon

100 g/3½ oz. feta cheese, crumbled

sea salt and freshly ground black pepper, to season

*a 20 x 30-cm/8 x 12-inch baking pan,*

**SERVES 4–6**

Mix the flour, yeast and fine salt in a large bowl. Add 1 tablespoon of the olive oil and the water and mix to a dough. Dust a work surface with flour and knead the dough on it for 10 minutes or until smooth and elastic. Shape the dough into a neat, smooth ball, return to the bowl and cover with clingfilm/plastic wrap. Let rise in a warm place for 1 hour or until double in size. Lightly oil the baking pan. Dust the work surface with flour, tip the dough out and knead for 30 seconds. Roll into a rectangle to fit in the baking pan. Lay the dough inside the pan. Cover with oiled clingfilm/plastic wrap and let rise in a warm place for about 1 hour or until doubled in size. Preheat the oven to 220°C (425°F) Gas 7. Dimple the top of the dough with your fingertips, drizzle over the remaining olive oil and scatter the with rosemary

and salt flakes. Bake in the oven for 20 minutes or until golden and risen. Cool in the pan for 10 minutes, then transfer to a wire rack. Cut the focaccia into finger-width slices, toast both sides on a ridged stove-top griddle/grill pan, rub the garlic clove over the toasted bread and top with one of the following:

Garlic Mushrooms: Heat the oil and butter in a frying pan/skillet, add the shallot and cook over medium heat until translucent. Add the mushrooms, season, cook until tender and stir through the parsley. Pile on top of the toasted bread. Drizzle with olive oil and serve warm.

Mediterranean Tomatoes: Add the tomatoes, (bell) pepper, basil and olives to a bowl and gently stir through the mozzarella. Pile on top of the toasted bread. Drizzle with olive oil and serve warm.

Beans & Mint: Cook the beans and/or peas in lightly salted boiling water until tender. Drain and refresh under cold water. Drain well, then whizz in a food processor to a coarse purée. Stir in the mint, zest and feta and season. Pile on top of the toasted bread. Drizzle with olive oil and serve warm.

# THE PERFECT SPRITZ

**ice cubes**
**200 ml/³/₄ cup Campari (or Aperol)**
**600 ml/2¹/₂ cups Prosecco (or white wine)**
**300–400 ml/1¹/₄–1³/₄ cups sparkling water**

**MAKES 4**

Put lots of cubed (never crushed) ice into four large, chilled wine glasses.

Divide the Campari (or Aperol) and Prosecco (or white wine) among the glasses, then top up with the sparkling water. Serve immediately.

# NEGRONI

**crushed ice**
**180 ml/³/₄ cup Campari**
**180 ml/³/₄ cup gin**
**60 ml/¹/₄ cup Cinzano Rosso**
**orange slices, to serve**

**MAKES 4**

Fill four tall glasses with crushed ice. Divide the Campari among the glasses, then the gin. Add the Cinzano Rosso and stir.

Drop a slice of orange into each glass and serve.

Greeting people with an enthusiastic kiss on each cheek... Nipping around town on a Vespa moped... Making a simple T-shirt and pair of jeans look effortlessly chic... The Italians have many wonderful customs and habits. But none more wonderful than the love of an aperitivo. Serve one (or all three!) of these bellissimo bubbly beverages as a pre-dinner warm-up to whet your guests' appetites and tease their taste buds. Saluti!

# TINTORETTO

**140 ml/¹/₂ cup pomegranate juice**
**600 ml/2¹/₂ cups Prosecco**

**MAKES 4**

Pour the pomegranate juice into four chilled Champagne flutes, then top up with the Prosecco. Serve at once.

# CHINESE NEW YEAR FESTIVITY

It'll be the year (or night) of the dumpling in your home as you serve up these packages of pure pow, along with nom-nom noodles, slurp-tastic soup and eat-me-now egg tarts. The colour red symbolizes joy and good fortune in Chinese culture, so paint your dining room red with Chinese lanterns, flowers, fans, parasols and perhaps even a dragon hung from the wall to oversee the evening's fun, fiery frolics.

## SMALL PLATES & SIDES

Steamed Rice Noodle Dumplings with Scallops
Sichuan Chilli Dressing
Mushroom-Filled Lettuce Cups
Flowering Chinese Prawns

## BIGGER BITES

Chicken Noodle Soup
Egg Noodle, Black Cloud Ear Fungus & Tofu Salad

## SOMETHING SWEET

Hong Kong Egg Tarts

# STEAMED RICE NOODLE DUMPLINGS WITH SCALLOPS

250 g/½ lb. scallops (without corals)
50 g/1¾ oz. (about 6) water chestnuts,
    drained and chopped
2 garlic cloves, crushed
1 tablespoon freshly chopped
    Chinese chives
1 tablespoon light soy sauce
2 teaspoons oyster sauce
1 teaspoon sesame oil
24 wonton wrappers
3–4 tablespoons sunflower oil
Sichuan Chilli Dressing (see recipe below)
spring onions/scallions, thinly sliced,
    to garnish

*a baking sheet lined with parchment paper*
*a medium bamboo steamer*

**SERVES 4**

Begin by preparing the scallops, cutting away the grey muscle attached at one side, and chop into small cubes. Put the scallop meat into a bowl with the water chestnuts, garlic, Chinese chives, soy sauce, oyster sauce and sesame oil, and stir to mix.

Lay the wonton wrappers flat on a board and place a teaspoon of the scallop mixture in the centre. Brush around the edges with a little water and draw the sides up and around the filling, pressing the edges together to seal. Transfer each one to the prepared baking sheet.

Dip the base of each dumpling into the sunflower oil and transfer to the bamboo steamer. Cover and steam over a pan of simmering water for 10–12 minutes until firm and cooked through.

Serve with the dressing, garnished with the thinly sliced spring onions/scallions.

# SICHUAN CHILLI DRESSING

100 ml/⅓ cup sunflower oil
1–2 teaspoons dried chilli/hot red
    pepper flakes
2 tablespoons light soy sauce
1 tablespoon black vinegar
2 teaspoons caster/granulated sugar
¼ teaspoon Sichuan peppercorns

**MAKES 200 ML/¾ CUP**

Heat the oil in a small saucepan set over medium heat until it just starts to shimmer. Remove from the heat and stir in the dried chilli/hot red pepper flakes. Set aside for 30 minutes, then strain through a fine-mesh sieve/strainer into a clean bowl. Stir in the remaining ingredients and serve as required.

Note: If you are making this dressing ahead of time, omit the peppercorns and add just before serving.

# EGG NOODLE, BLACK CLOUD EAR FUNGUS & TOFU SALAD

15 g/1½ cup dried black cloud ear fungus
200 g/7 oz. fresh egg noodles
½ cucumber, peeled
1 large carrot
150 g/6 oz. marinated tofu, thinly sliced
4 spring onions/scallions, thinly sliced
100 g/1⅓ cups sliced Chinese cabbage/
   Napa cabbage, sliced
a small handful each of mint
   and coriander/cilantro
1 tablespoon sesame seeds, toasted

DRESSING
2 tablespoons light soy sauce
2 tablespoons brown rice vinegar
1 tablespoon caster/granulated sugar
1 teaspoon sesame oil
1 teaspoon chilli/chili oil

SERVES 4

Put the black cloud ear fungus in a large mixing bowl, cover with boiling water and soak for 20 minutes until softened. Drain well, pat dry with paper towels and slice thinly, discarding any tough stems. Set aside.

Meanwhile, cook the noodles by plunging them into a saucepan of boiling water. Return to a boil and simmer for 2–3 minutes until al dente. Drain and immediately refresh under cold water before draining again. Dry thoroughly using a clean tea/kitchen towel and set aside.

Cut the cucumber and carrot into thin strips and place in a large mixing bowl. Add the black cloud ear fungus, tofu, spring onions/scallions, cabbage and herbs and toss well.

To make the dressing, beat all the ingredients together in a small bowl until the sugar is dissolved.

Stir the noodles into the salad, add the dressing and toss well until evenly combined. Serve in bowls, sprinkled with the sesame seeds.

# MUSHROOM-FILLED LETTUCE CUPS

1 tablespoon vegetable oil
1-cm/½-inch piece of fresh root ginger,
   peeled and finely chopped
1 garlic clove, finely chopped
2 spring onions/scallions, finely chopped,
   white and green separated
300 g/10½ oz. white mushrooms
1 tablespoon Shaoxing rice wine or pale
   dry sherry
2 teaspoons light soy sauce
1 tablespoon oyster sauce
8 even-sized Little Gem/Bibb lettuce leaves
coriander/cilantro leaves, to garnish
finely chopped red chilli/chile, to garnish

MAKES 8

Heat the oil in a wok or large frying pan/skillet. Add the ginger, garlic and white spring onion/scallion and stir-fry over medium heat for 1 minute.

Dice the mushrooms into 1-cm/½-inch pieces and stir-fry for 2 minutes. Add the rice wine or sherry and stir-fry for 1 minute, until cooked off. Add the soy sauce and oyster sauce. Stir-fry for 2 minutes. Toss through the green spring onion/scallion.

While the mushroom mixture is hot or at room temperature, spoon it into the lettuce leaves, filling each one with the mixture. Garnish with coriander/cilantro leaves and finely chopped red chilli/chile and serve at once.

# CHICKEN NOODLE SOUP

200 g/7 oz. dried
   Hokkien noodles
1.25 litres/5¼ cups
   chicken stock
2 teaspoons grated fresh
   root ginger
2 tablespoons light
   soy sauce
2 tablespoons Shaoxing
   rice wine or pale dry
   sherry
1 tablespoon oyster sauce
200 g/1½ cups sliced
   chicken breast fillet

250 g/½ lb. or about
   6 whole pak choi/bok
   choy, roughly chopped
2 spring onions/scallions,
   thinly sliced, plus extra
   to serve
salt, to season

TO GARNISH (OPTIONAL)
fresh chillies/chiles, sliced
a small bunch of
   coriander/cilantro

**SERVES 4**

Plunge the noodles into a saucepan of boiling
water and cook for 3–4 minutes until al dente. Drain,
refresh under cold water and shake dry. Set aside.

Pour the stock into a large saucepan with the
ginger, soy sauce, rice wine and oyster sauce and set
over medium heat. Bring slowly to the boil, then
simmer for 5 minutes.

Stir in the chicken, pak choi/bok choy and spring
onions/scallions and simmer for 3–4 minutes until
the chicken is cooked.

Divide the noodles between bowls, pour over the
chicken soup and serve garnished with some sliced
chillies/chiles and coriander/cilantro, if you like.

Note: If using fresh Hokkien noodles, cook for
2 minutes instead of 3–4. If using vacuum-packed,
pre-cooked noodles, rinse under boiling water only
before use. For either you will need 500 g/1 lb. 2 oz.

# FLOWERING CHINESE PRAWNS

1 tablespoon sunflower or
   vegetable oil
2-cm/¾-inch piece of fresh
   root ginger, peeled and
   finely sliced
200 g/7 oz. flowering
   Chinese chives or
   Chinese chives, chopped
   into 2.5-cm/1-inch
   lengths

200 g/7 oz. raw prawns/
   shrimp, peeled
1 tablespoon Shaoxing rice
   wine or pale dry sherry
1 tablespoon light
   soy sauce
½ teaspoon sesame oil

**SERVES 2**

Place the oil in a wok over high heat. Add the
ginger and stir-fry for 1 minute until fragrant. Next
put in the Chinese chives and stir-fry briefly.

Add the prawns/shrimp and stir-fry. As soon as
the prawns/shrimp turn opaque, add the rice wine
or sherry and sizzle briefly. Lastly, add the soy sauce
and sesame oil. Stir-fry for 2–3 minutes until the
Chinese chives are just wilted. Serve at once, with
noodles if you like.

# HONG KONG EGG TARTS

**PUFF PASTRY**
**Water dough:**
100 g/³/₄ cup Asian white wheat flour,
   plus extra for dusting
1 heaped tablespoon caster/superfine sugar
40 ml/3 tablespoons water
30 g/2 tablespoons unsalted butter, melted

**Butter dough:**
100 g/³/₄ cup Asian white wheat flour
50 g/3¹/₂ tablespoons unsalted butter,
   melted

**EGG TART**
100 ml/¹/₃ cup milk
50 g/¹/₄ cup caster/superfine sugar
2 eggs
seeds from 1 vanilla pod/bean

*a small round fluted pastry cutter*
*12 individual mini tart pans*

**MAKES 12**

First, make the puff pastry. In a large mixing bowl, combine the ingredients for the water dough. Form the dough into a ball and knead lightly until smooth and silky. Wrap the dough with clingfilm/plastic wrap and rest in the fridge for 15 minutes. Divide the dough into 12 and roll each piece into a ball. Cover with a damp tea/kitchen towel and set aside. In a second mixing bowl, repeat the same full process with the butter dough ingredients, but instead of chilling, rest at room temperature for 15 minutes.

To assemble the dough, take a water dough ball and knead gently and briefly. Very lightly flour the worktop and use a rolling pin to roll out the ball of water dough to a diameter of 7.5 cm/3 inches. Place a butter dough ball in the centre and wrap the water dough around to enclose it completely. Turn the dough ball over so that the join is on the underside. Roll the combined dough into a thick square package. Fold the package into three and flatten with the rolling pin again. Repeat this fold and roll process twice with each ball. Cover and rest in the fridge for 15 minutes. In the meantime, prepare the egg tart filling.

Preheat the oven to 200°C (400°F) Gas 6.

Beat together the milk, sugar, eggs and vanilla seeds in a large bowl until the sugar has fully dissolved. Pass the mixture twice through a sieve/strainer to make it as smooth as possible.

Roll out each chilled dough ball and use the cutter to stamp out circles of dough to fit the mini tart pans. Lay a circle of dough in the tart pan and prick the base with a fork. Repeat for all 12 dough balls. Let the tart cases/shells chill in the fridge for 5 minutes.

Pour the egg mixture into the tart cases/shells to come three-quarters of the way up the sides and bake in the preheated oven for 10 minutes. Lower the oven temperature to 170°C (325°F) Gas 3 and bake for an additional 10 minutes. Let cool on a wire rack before serving.

# SPANISH TAPAS
# &
# SANGRIA TASTING

Convert your casa into a buzzing tapas bar serving an array of appetizing Spanish small-plate classics. Prior to your guests arriving, you may want to prepare yourself with a little 'Spanish yoga', also known as a siesta, so that you've got the energy to entertain – and eat – into the small hours. Plus you'll need all the stamina you can get as you dip into the decadent churros.

## SMALL PLATES & SIDES
Manchego & Olive Pinchos
Patatas Bravas
Ham & Chicken Croquettes
Chorizo in Red Wine

## BIGGER BITES
Spanish Potato Tortilla

## SOMETHING SWEET
Churros

## DRINKS
Sangria Straight-Up

## PATATAS BRAVAS

300 g/10½ oz. waxy
   potatoes, peeled
2 tablespoons olive oil
1 shallot, chopped
1 garlic clove, chopped
1 dried chilli/chile
1 tablespoon sherry
   vinegar
1 x 400-g/14-oz. can
   plum tomatoes

1 teaspoon hot smoked
   paprika/pimentón
salt and freshly ground
   black pepper, to season
chopped parsley,
   to garnish

**SERVES 4**

Boil the potatoes in salted boiling water until just tender; drain, cool and dice.

Meanwhile, prepare the spicy tomato sauce. Heat 1 tablespoon of the oil in a small, heavy-bottomed frying pan/skillet. Add the shallot and garlic and crumble in the dried chilli/chile. Fry, stirring, for 1–2 minutes until fragrant. Add the sherry vinegar and continue to cook for 1 minute until syrupy. Add the canned tomatoes and mix well. Season with salt and pepper and add the smoked paprika/pimentón. Turn up the heat and bring to a boil. Cook the sauce uncovered, stirring often to break down the tomatoes, for 10–15 minutes until reduced and slightly thickened.

In a separate large frying pan/skillet, heat the remaining olive oil. Add the cooled, diced potatoes and fry until golden brown on all sides, stirring often and seasoning with salt. Pour the cooked tomato sauce over the potatoes, garnish with chopped parsley and serve hot or at room temperature.

## MANCHEGO & OLIVE PINCHOS

125 ml/½ cup extra virgin
   olive oil
1 small orange, quartered
   and sliced
8 garlic cloves, peeled
3 rosemary sprigs
few pinches of sea salt flakes
2 x 200-g/7-oz. wedges

young Manchego cheese,
   cut into shards, 2 cm/
   ¾ inch at its widest end
about 40 pimiento-stuffed
   Manzanilla olives

*20 cocktail sticks/toothpicks*

**MAKES ABOUT 20**

Stir the oil, orange and garlic in a saucepan over low–medium heat for 10–12 minutes. Remove from the heat and add the rosemary. Season with the salt, cool, then pour into a bowl. Add the cheese and toss to coat. Cover and chill in the fridge for 8 hours. To assemble, drain the cheese on paper towels. Thread two olives and a Manchego shard onto a cocktail stick/toothpick and serve.

# HAM & CHICKEN CROQUETTES

250 ml/1 cup milk
½ small onion, sliced
1 bay leaf
2 black peppercorns
thyme sprig of fresh
30 g/2 tablespoons
    unsalted butter
3 tablespoons plain/
    all-purpose flour
a pinch of oak-smoked
    sweet Spanish paprika
a pinch of freshly grated
    nutmeg

oil, for frying and
    deep-frying
150 g/5½ oz. Serrano ham,
    finely chopped
100 g/3½ oz. cooked
    chicken breast, finely
    chopped
300 g/2¾ cups dried
    breadcrumbs
2 eggs, lightly beaten

**SERVES 4**

Put the milk in a saucepan, add the onion, bay leaf, pepper and thyme and heat until just below boiling point. Remove from the heat, let cool, then strain into a bowl.

Melt the butter in a saucepan, stir in the flour and cook for 2 minutes, stirring constantly. Slowly add the milk, stirring to deter lumps. Continue to cook, adding the paprika and nutmeg.

Heat 1 tablespoon oil in a frying pan/skillet, add the ham and sauté until the fat starts to run. Add the ham and chicken to the white sauce and cook until the sauce thickens, about 2 minutes.

Remove from the heat to cool. Cover and refrigerate for at least 3 hours. Shape the cooled mixture into 6 x 2-cm/2½ x 1-inch croquettes. Roll in the breadcrumbs, dip into the beaten eggs and roll in the breadcrumbs again. Cover and chill for 1 hour or overnight.

Fill a large saucepan or deep-fat fryer one-third full of oil or to the manufacturer's recommended level and heat to 190°C (375°F) or until a cube of bread browns in 30 seconds. Add the in small batches croquettes and fry for 3 minutes or until golden brown. Remove and drain on paper towels.

# SANGRIA STRAIGHT-UP

25 ml/¾ fl. oz. Spanish
    brandy
1 x 750-ml bottle fruity red
    wine
45 ml/1½ fl. oz. sugar
    syrup
45 ml/1½ fl. oz. any
    orange-flavoured
    liqueur, such as curaçao,
    triple sec, Cointreau or
    Grand Marnier
freshly squeezed juice of ½
    orange

freshly squeezed juice
    of ½ lemon
ice chips or crushed ice,
    to serve

TO GARNISH
small orange and lemon
    half-moons
mint sprigs (optional)

12 small tumblers

**MAKES 12**

Mix all of the ingredients together in a jug/pitcher. Strain into ice-chip- or crushed-ice-filled serving glasses. Garnish each one with an orange and lemon slice and a mint sprig (if you like) and serve.

# SPANISH POTATO TORTILLA

250 ml/1 cup olive oil
300 g/10½ oz. waxy
   potatoes, peeled,
   quartered and thinly
   sliced
1 onion, halved and thinly
   sliced
6 UK large/US extra-large
   eggs

salt and freshly ground
   black pepper, to season

a 16-cm/6¼-inch heavy-
   bottomed frying pan/
   skillet

**SERVES 4–6 AS PART
OF A TAPAS SPREAD,
OR 2 FOR A MEAL**

Pour the olive oil into the frying pan/skillet. Add in
the sliced potatoes and onion, cover the pan and
cook gently over low heat until softened but not
coloured, stirring now and then. In effect, you're
stewing the vegetables in the oil.

While the potatoes are cooking, beat together the
eggs in a bowl and season with salt and pepper.

Strain the potato mixture into a colander, reserving
the olive oil for future use. Season the potato
mixture lightly with salt and pour the hot vegetables
into the beaten eggs, gently mixing together.

Heat 1 tablespoon of the reserved oil in the same
frying pan/skillet. Add in the egg mixture and fry
gently for 10–15 minutes until it has set and there is
just a small pool of liquid egg on the surface.

Cover the frying pan/skillet with a plate that is larger
than the pan and tip over the frying pan/skillet so as
to invert the tortilla onto the plate. Gently slide the
tortilla back into the frying pan/skillet and cook for
an additional 2 minutes to set the other side.
Remove from the pan and serve warm or at room
temperature.

# CHORIZO IN RED WINE

1 tablespoon olive oil
300 g/10½ oz. small, spicy
   cooking chorizo
   sausages, cut into
   1-cm/½-inch slices

100 ml/⅓ cup red wine
crusty bread, to serve

**SERVES 4**

Put the oil in a heavy-bottomed frying pan/skillet
and heat until smoking. Add the chorizo and cook for
1 minute. Reduce the heat, add the wine and cook for
5 minutes. Transfer to a serving dish and set aside to
develop the flavours. Serve warm with crusty bread.

Sometimes referred to as Spanish doughnuts, churros are traditionally scarfed in Spain for breakfast (sure beats a bowl of muesli) or as a mid-morning snack. Hot chocolate is the dipping 'sauce' and sometimes they're sprinkled with sugar. Mmm! Unless you're planning on your dinner party becoming a sleepover, serve your churros as a delectable dessert (this sauce is waaaay thicker than a hot chocolate) that your friends can share. One taste and all etiquette relating to double-dipping will go out the window as everyone dips and devours with abandon.

# CHURROS

½ teaspoon salt
200 g/1½ cups strong white/bread flour
¼ teaspoon bicarbonate of soda/baking soda
260 ml/generous 1 cup water at around 70°C (160°F)
400 ml/1¾ cups sunflower/corn oil, for frying

DIPPING SAUCE
100 g/3½ oz. dark/bittersweet (70%) chocolate, chopped
120 ml/½ cup double/heavy cream

a thermometer
a piping/pastry bag fitted with a star nozzle/ tip (optional)

MAKES ABOUT 30

Beat together the salt, flour and bicarbonate of soda/baking soda in a bowl. Add the water and beat quite vigorously so that there are no lumps. Let sit in the bowl while you prepare the oil.

Heat the oil in a small saucepan and bring to 180°C (350°F).

Spoon the dough into a piping/pastry bag (fit it with a star nozzle/ tip if you want ridges). Twist the piping/pastry bag and hold with one hand. Gently squeeze out the dough to a 5-cm/2-inch piece and snip with scissors into the oil, frying in small batches.

Fry for a couple of minutes and then turn over with tongs and cook until golden brown. Drain on paper towels and keep the fried churros warm in a low oven.

There is no strict shape for churros. Snipping them into the hot oil in lines is the easiest way to get started. Once you get the hang of it, you can try piping them into other shapes, such as the horseshoes shown.

For the dipping sauce, place the chopped chocolate in a heatproof bowl. Bring the double/heavy cream to a simmer in a saucepan, then pour over the chocolate. Let it sit for 1 minute, then stir to combine. Serve the churros immediately, accompanied by the dipping sauce.

# MOREISH MEZZE

Host your very own Arabian night and take your guests' senses
on a journey to remember with this magnificent mezze spread. They'll
feast their eyes – and then their tummies – on your mouth-watering
offerings, which bring the colours, smells and tastes of this magical part
of the world to life. Encourage them to linger over your zingy dip, fruity
cocktail and pastry as they've never savoured it before, which
will not only surprise, but also delight.

## SMALL PLATES & SIDES

Little Spinach & Feta Pastries
Falafel with Tzatziki
Baba Ghanoush

## BIGGER BITES

Greek Rice-Stuffed Tomatoes

## SOMETHING SWEET

Shredded Pastry with Cheese in Lemon Syrup

## DRINKS

Rose & Pomegranate Cosmo

# LITTLE SPINACH & FETA PASTRIES

500 g/1 lb. 2 oz. spinach
　leaves, trimmed
2 tablespoons olive oil,
　plus extra for brushing
15 g/1 tablespoon butter
2 onions, chopped
3 heaped tablespoons
　pine nuts (reserve
　1 tablespoon for
　garnishing)
juice of 1 lemon
1 teaspoon ground allspice
150 g/5½ oz. feta cheese,

crumbled with your
　fingers
1 small bunch of dill, finely
　chopped
plain/all-purpose flour,
　for dusting
450 g/16 oz. ready-
　prepared puff pastry
sea salt and freshly ground
　black pepper, to season

*a 10-cm/4-inch round*
*pastry cutter or cup*

**SERVES 6**

Preheat the oven to 180°C (350°F) Gas 4.

Steam the spinach until soft and floppy, then drain, refresh under running cold water and squeeze out the excess liquid with your hands. Place the spinach on a wooden board and chop it coarsely.

Heat the oil and butter in a heavy-bottomed pan and stir in the onions to soften. Add the pine nuts and cook for 2–3 minutes until both begin to turn golden. Stir in the spinach, lemon juice and allspice and lightly toss in the crumbled feta and dill. Season the mixture with a little salt and pepper and let cool.

Lightly dust a surface with flour and thinly roll out the pastry. Using the pastry cutter or cup's rim, cut out as many circles as you can, lightly dusting with flour. Take each circle and spoon a little of the spinach mixture in the middle. Pull up the sides to make a pyramid by pinching the edges with your fingertips – it does not matter if one of the sides opens during cooking, as that is part of the appeal.

Lightly oil two baking sheets and place the pastries on them. Brush the tops with a little oil and bake them in the preheated oven for about 30 minutes, until golden brown.

Roughly 5 minutes before taking the pastries out of the oven, spread the reserved tablespoon of pine nuts onto a small piece of aluminium foil and toast them in the oven until they turn golden brown. Once you have placed the little pastries on a plate, sprinkle the toasted pine nuts over them and serve while they are still hot.

# GREEK RICE-STUFFED TOMATOES

4–6 large tomatoes
3 tablespoons olive oil
1 small onion, finely
　chopped
150 g/¾ cup long-grain
　rice, rinsed
1 teaspoon tomato
　purée/paste
2 tablespoons chopped
　flat-leaf parsley

2 tablespoons chopped dill
2 tablespoons chopped
　mint
1 teaspoon grated
　lemon zest
salt and freshly ground
　black pepper, to season

**SERVES 4**

Preheat the oven to 200°C (400°F) Gas 6.

Cut the tomato tops. Scoop out and reserve the soft pulp. Put the tomato shells upright in a large baking dish. Set aside with the caps until ready to bake.

Heat 2 tablespoons of the oil in a frying pan/skillet over low heat. Add the onion and fry until softened. Add the reserved tomato pulp, rice and tomato purée/paste. Season with salt and pepper. Bring the mixture to a boil and cook for 10 minutes, stirring often. Stir in the herbs and lemon zest.

Fill the tomato shells with the rice mixture and add the tops. Drizzle with the remaining oil, cover with foil and oven-bake for 1 hour until the rice is tender.

# FALAFEL WITH TZATZIKI

**FALAFEL**
225 g/1 cup dried chickpeas
1 small red onion, peeled
3 garlic cloves, peeled
2 tablespoons ground
    coriander
2 tablespoons ground
    cumin
1 large bunch coriander/
    cilantro
1 large bunch flat-leaf
    parsley
2 slices rustic white bread,
    crusts removed
4 tablespoons olive oil
vegetable oil, for frying

sea salt and freshly ground
    black pepper, to season

**TZATZIKI**
1 cucumber
350 g/1½ cups natural/
    plain thick Greek yogurt
juice of ½ lemon
1 small bunch mint,
    chopped
1 garlic clove, crushed
sea salt

*a deep-fat fryer*

MAKES 20–30

Rinse the chickpeas, then let soak in plenty of water overnight.

Once soaked, put the chickpeas, along with all the other falafel ingredients except the vegetable oil in a food processor and blend to a rough paste. Avoid the temptation of blending it too much; the falafel should still have texture when you bite into it.

Heat the vegetable oil to 180°C (350°F) in a deep-fat fryer. Take 2 dessertspoons of falafel mix and shape them into a quenelle or ball shape. Fry the falafels in batches in the hot oil until they are very dark brown (they will colour quickly, but avoid the temptation to remove them from the oil too soon; they need to fry for at least 3–4 minutes in order to crisp up properly). Remove and let cool on a wire rack.

For the tzatziki, cut the cucumber in half lengthways. Use a teaspoon to scoop out the seeds and discard. Grate the rest of the cucumber, then mix with a little salt and let drain in a colander for 10 minutes to remove the excess liquid. Stir the yogurt, lemon juice, mint and garlic into the cucumber.

Season with extra salt if necessary, and serve with the falafel.

# BABA GHANOUSH

4 aubergines/eggplants
2 garlic cloves, crushed
1 generous tablespoon
    tahini paste
juice of 1 lemon
2–3 tablespoons olive oil,
    plus extra for greasing
sea salt and ground
    black pepper, to season

a sprinkling of
    pomegranate seeds,
    chopped coriander/
    cilantro, ½ teaspoon
    toasted cumin seeds or
    a teaspoon of harissa
    paste, to garnish
Flatbreads (see page 127),
    to serve

SERVES 6

Preheat the oven to 200°C (400°F) Gas 6.

Put the aubergines/eggplants on an oiled baking sheet and roast in the preheated oven for about 30 minutes or until the skins are blistered and blackened. Remove from the oven and let cool.

Scrape all the flesh from the aubergines/eggplants into a mixing bowl, discarding the skins. Add the garlic, tahini, most of the lemon juice and 2 tablespoons of the olive oil. Using a fork, mash the flesh into a chunky purée. Season with a pinch of salt and pepper. If the paste is too thick or the taste of garlic is too strong, add a little more lemon juice and olive oil.

Sprinkle your chosen garnish on top, drizzle with a little olive oil and serve with the warm flatbreads.

## SHREDDED PASTRY WITH CHEESE IN LEMON SYRUP

225 g/½ lb. ready-prepared
  kadaif (finely shredded
  filo/phyllo pastry)
120 g/½ cup ghee, melted
350 g/12 oz. dil peyniri or
  mozzarella cheese,
  thinly sliced
1–2 tablespoons
  shelled pistachios,
  coarsely ground

SYRUP
225 g/1 cup plus
  2 tablespoons
  granulated sugar
125 ml/½ cup water
juice of 1 lemon

*a shallow baking pan*

**SERVES 4–6**

Preheat the oven to 180°C (350°F) Gas 4.

First prepare the syrup. Put the sugar and water into a pan and bring it to a boil, stirring until the sugar has dissolved. Add the lemon juice, reduce the heat, and let the syrup simmer and thicken for about 15 minutes until it coats the back of a wooden spoon. Turn off the heat and let the syrup cool. Chill it in the fridge if you like.

Put the kadaif into a bowl and separate the strands. Pour the melted ghee over them and, using your fingers, rub it all over the strands so that they are coated in it. Spread half the pastry in the bottom of your baking pan (the Turks use a round pan roughly 27 cm/11 inches in diameter) and press it down with your fingers. Lay the slices of cheese over the top and cover with the rest of the pastry, pressing it down firmly and tucking it down the sides.

Place the pan in the preheated oven and bake the pastry for about 45 minutes until it is golden brown. Loosen the edges of the pastry with a sharp knife and pour the cold syrup over it – the hot pastry will absorb most of the syrup, but you can pop it back into the oven for 2–3 minutes to ensure that it does. Scatter the pistachios over the top. Divide the pastry into squares or segments, depending on the shape of your baking pan, and serve while still hot, so that the cheese remains soft.

## ROSE & POMEGRANATE COSMO

35 ml/1¼ fl. oz. vodka
20 ml/⅔ fl. oz. triple sec
20 ml/⅔ fl. oz. freshly
  squeezed lemon juice
25 ml/1 fl. oz. pomegranate
  juice
1 teaspoon agave nectar
½ teaspoon rosewater

ice cubes
fresh rose petals,
  to garnish

*2 fridge-frosted mini
  martini glasses*

**MAKES 2**

Add all the ingredients to a cocktail shaker filled with ice cubes. Shake until chilled and then strain into the chilled mini martini glasses. Garnish with rose petals.

# SCANDI FISH AFFAIR

Hide your clutter, then grab your most understated-yet-stylish
table runner, a few chunky, white candles and some inner calm as you
invite your guests to get their hygge on in the comfort of your serene
Scandi-esque home. Your evening will radiate happiness and contentment,
with wellness and excellent taste being the focus of this veritable
smörgåsbord of delicious. Because enjoying good food in good
company is one of life's simple pleasures.

## SMALL PLATES & SIDES
Mustard Herring
Dill & Apple Herring
Creamy Potato Salad

## BIGGER BITES
Gravad Lax
Black Rice & Salmon Salad

## SOMETHING SWEET
Blueberry Tart with Rye

## DRINKS
Homemade Dill Aquavit

# MUSTARD HERRING

150 g/5½ oz. (drained
    weight) plain pickled
    herring
2 tablespoons Swedish
    wholegrain mustard
    (or a grainy sweet
    mustard will work)
1 teaspoon Dijon mustard
1 tablespoon caster/
    granulated sugar
2 tablespoons white wine
    vinegar
2 tablespoons double/
    heavy cream
1 tablespoon crème
    fraîche/sour cream

1 small shallot, finely
    chopped
100 ml/⅓ cup plus
    1 tablespoon sunflower
    or other neutral oil
2 tablespoons finely
    chopped dill
1 tablespoon chopped
    chives (optional)
salt and freshly ground
    black pepper, to season
rye bread or crisp bread,
    to serve

**SERVES 4**

Drain the herring and discard the brine and any
onion bits.

In a bowl, mix everything together except the oil,
herbs and herring. Slowly pour in the oil while
beating continuously so that the sauce emulsifies.

Stir in the herbs, then the herring. Cover and
refrigerate for a few hours to marinate, then serve
with rye bread or crispbread.

# GRAVAD LAX

1 whole salmon fillet,
    about 600 g/1¼ lbs.,
    skin on
2 tablespoons coarse
    sea salt
1 teaspoon caster/
    granulated sugar

a handful of dill,
    torn into small sprigs
2 tablespoons Cognac
    (optional)

**MAKES 1 WHOLE
SALMON GRAVAD LAX**

Place the fillet on a large sheet of greaseproof/wax
paper, skinside down. Sprinkle the salt and sugar
evenly over the surface. Scatter the dill on top.
Drizzle over the Cognac, if using.

Wrap the paper very tightly around the salmon. Take
another sheet of greaseproof/wax paper and wrap
that tightly around the salmon too. Place on a dish,
skinside down, and refrigerate for 24 hours. Turn
over after 12 hours.

For two open sandwiches spread 1 tablespoon
mayonnaise over 1 slice of rye bread, sliced in half.
Top with 50 g/1¾ oz. thinly sliced Gravad Lax,
4 very thin slices of cucumber and a small handful
of roughly chopped dill.

# DILL & APPLE HERRING

50 ml/3½ tablespoons
    mayonnaise
100 ml/⅓ cup crème
    fraîche/sour cream
1 teaspoon Dijon mustard
1 teaspoon honey
squeeze of lemon juice,
    to taste
3 tablespoons finely
    chopped chives
3 tablespoons freshly
    chopped dill

½ red apple, cut into
    small cubes
150 g/5½ oz. (drained
    weight) onion-pickled
    herring, cut into
    bite-sized pieces
salt and freshly ground
    black pepper, to season
chopped red onion and
    whole dill sprigs,
    to garnish

**SERVES 4**

In a bowl, mix together the mayonnaise, crème
fraîche/sour cream and mustard. Add the honey, salt
and pepper and lemon juice and then fold in the
chopped chives and dill. Finally, add the apple and
then the herring at the end.

Cover and refrigerate for a few hours to let the
flavours mingle. Garnish with chopped red onion and
dill sprigs.

# BLACK RICE & SALMON SALAD

200 g/1 cup uncooked
   black rice
1 cucumber
1 green apple
1 shallot, finely chopped
squeeze of lemon juice
1 bunch of dill, chopped
2 tablespoons freshly
   chopped parsley
1 tablespoon chopped mint
   (optional)
150 g/5½ oz. hot-smoked
   salmon

DRESSING
2 tablespoons white wine
   vinegar
4 tablespoons good-
   quality olive or
   rapeseed/canola oil
1 tablespoon honey
1 tablespoon freshly
   squeezed lemon or
   lime juice (plus extra as
   needed)
salt and freshly ground
   black pepper, to season

**SERVES 4 OR 6–7 AS
A SIDE**

Rinse the black rice a few times, then bring to
a boil in a large pan of water. Cook until al dente
following the package instructions (it can take about
30 minutes to cook, a bit like brown rice). Once
cooked, rinse well to remove the excess colour. Drain
and let cool.

Slice the cucumber lengthways, then scrape out
the seeds and chop into 5-mm/¼-inch pieces. Chop
the apple into similarly sized small pieces. Add the
cucumber, apple and shallot to a serving bowl with
a squeeze of lemon juice to keep the apple fresh.
Add the cooked and cooled black rice, dill, parsley
and mint, if using. Flake in the salmon and mix
gently to combine everything together.

Beat together the dressing ingredients in a small
bowl and season to taste. Pour the dressing over the
salad and stir. Do adjust the seasoning once you have
done this – it may need more lemon juice or even a
squeeze of lime (this depends on the saltiness of the
fish and the sweetness of the apple you have used).

# CREAMY POTATO SALAD

500–600 g/about 1¼ lbs.
   cooked skin-on new
   potatoes, cold and cut
   into bite-sized pieces

CREAMY DRESSING
75 g/⅓ cup natural/plain
   Greek-style yogurt
75 g/⅓ cup mayonnaise
1 teaspoon Dijon mustard

4 spring onions/scallions,
   sliced
50 g/⅓ cup chopped
   pickled cucumber/dill
   pickles
6–7 radishes, sliced
sea salt and freshly ground
   black pepper, to season

**SERVES 4 AS A SIDE**

Mix everything together, cover and refrigerate
for a few hours for the flavours to mingle before
serving. If you need more zing, add pickle juice
or lemon juice.

# BLUEBERRY TART WITH RYE

100 g/7 tablespoons
   unsalted butter,
   softened at room
   temperature
85 g/scant ½ cup
   caster/superfine sugar
1 egg, lightly beaten
100 g/¾ cup plain/
   all-purpose flour
60 g/½ cup wholemeal
   rye flour
1 teaspoon baking powder

**FILLING**
100 g/⅓ cup crème fraîche
150 ml/⅔ cup sour/soured
   cream
1 egg, lightly beaten
40 g/3 tablespoons
   caster/superfine sugar
1 teaspoon vanilla extract
250 g/1¾ cups blueberries

*a 24-cm/9½-inch
   fluted tart pan with a
   removable base, greased*

**SERVES 6–8**

Preheat the oven to 200°C (400°F) Gas 6.

Put the butter and sugar in a mixing bowl and beat until well mixed. Gradually add the egg, mixing well. Tip in the flours and baking powder and mix again until a dough has formed.

Transfer the dough to the prepared tart pan and push and press it into the pan until the bottom and sides are evenly covered with a neat layer of dough.

To make the filling, put the crème fraîche, sour/soured cream, egg, sugar and vanilla extract in a mixing bowl and mix well. Pour into the pastry case/shell, then scatter the blueberries into the tart.

Bake in the preheated oven for 25 minutes or until the filling has set and the pastry is golden brown.

# HOMEMADE DILL AQUAVIT

1 bunch of dill
1 teaspoon white sugar
350 ml/1½ cups vodka,
   plus extra to taste

*a large sterilized Mason/
   Kilner jar and glass bottle
a coffee filter*

**MAKES AROUND
350 ML/12 FL OZ.**

Blanch the dill in boiling water for a few seconds, then shake dry and add to the jar (blanching fresh herbs before adding gives a stronger taste).

Add the sugar, then top up with vodka and stir. Seal the jar and let stand at room temperature for 5–6 days.

Strain through the coffee filter to remove the dill. Decant into the bottle and keep for another month before topping up with more vodka to taste. Serve chilled in shot glasses.

# MEAT FEAST

A ham sarnie, chicken drumsticks and spag Bol those dishes ain't. Not that there's anything wrong with those simple meaty treats... but for your Big Meaty Night In, you'd be doing yourself – and your dining companions – a disservice if you didn't opt for something a bit fancier. Think delectable duck, gratifying gratin, I'm-salivating salumi, swish Scotch eggs, chow-down chorizo and kebabs/kebobs with kapow. Bring on the meat sweats!

## SMALL PLATES & SIDES
Cured Duck & Mustard Bruschetta
Salumi Chips
'Scotch Eggs'

## BIGGER BITES
Chorizo & Red Cabbage Salad
Cured Pork Kebab Skewers
Tomato Bacon Gratin

# CURED DUCK & MUSTARD BRUSCHETTA

1 baguette
1 garlic clove, peeled
olive oil, for drizzling
about 2 teaspoons
    wholegrain mustard
    (Dijon/French or
English/hot mustard
    also work well)
a handful of rocket/
    arugula leaves
12 slices cured duck breast

**MAKES 4**

Preheat the grill/broiler to medium. Slice the baguette diagonally into 1-cm/½-inch slices. Rub the garlic clove around the edge of the baguette slices – the hard crust will rub the flavour off the garlic clove without overpowering the bread.

Drizzle olive oil onto a baking sheet and then lay the baguette slices on top. Drizzle a little more olive oil over the top of the slices. Grill/broil for 4–5 minutes, turning halfway through.

Spread some mustard on each slice of bruschetta. Arrange a few leaves of rocket/arugula on top and layer the slices of cured meat over the top to serve.

# CHORIZO & RED CABBAGE SALAD

SALAD
1 tablespoon olive oil
½ red cabbage, cored and
    sliced or shredded
150 g/5½ oz. chorizo,
    peeled and diced

DRESSING
3 tablespoons olive oil
1 tablespoon red wine
    vinegar
½ teaspoon garlic purée or
    crushed garlic
a big pinch of chopped
    parsley
a pinch of chopped
    or dried tarragon
1 teaspoon freshly
    squeezed lime juice

**SERVES 4 AS A SIDE**

For the salad, heat the olive oil in a frying pan/skillet over medium heat, then add the red cabbage and fry until soft, stirring regularly.

Add the chorizo and keep stirring for 2–3 minutes so that the chorizo starts to cook and releases its oils.

Remove from the heat and let cool.

Meanwhile, put all the ingredients for the dressing into a bowl and mix together well.

Once the cabbage and chorizo mixture has cooled, pour over the dressing, toss to mix and serve.

# CURED PORK KEBAB SKEWERS

500 g/1 lbs. 2 oz. cured
  pork loin
2 shallots, chopped
1 teaspoon paprika
a pinch of chipotle powder
2 tablespoons sherry
1 teaspoon soft/packed
  brown sugar
a pinch of chopped fresh or
  dried parsley
a pinch each of sea salt
  and freshly ground black
  pepper
1 courgette/zucchini, sliced
1 Romano chilli/chile,
  seeded and sliced
1 tablespoon olive oil

SWEET & FEISTY CRÈME
  FRAÎCHE
2 tablespoons crème
  fraîche/sour cream
1 teaspoon chipotle chilli/
  chili powder
4 pinches of cayenne
  pepper
2 teaspoons maple syrup

*wooden skewers, soaked
  in water for at least
  30 minutes, or metal
  skewers*

**SERVES 2**

The day before serving, trim the pork loin to remove
any rind and unwanted fat on the top. Cut the pork
into large cubes, about 2 cm/³⁄₄ inch each. Set aside.

Put the shallots, paprika, chipotle powder, sherry,
sugar, parsley and salt and pepper into a food
processor and whizz together until mixed. Transfer
to a freezer bag with the pork pieces, toss together,
seal the bag and refrigerate overnight to marinate.

The next day, prepare the Sweet & Feisty Crème
Fraîche. Put the ingredients into a bowl and stir. Set
aside or cover and keep refrigerated for up to 2 days.

Thread the pork, the courgette/zucchini and Romano
chilli/chile slices alternating onto the skewers. Heat
a ridged stove-top griddle/grill pan over high heat
with the olive oil added. Cook the kebabs/kebobs in
the pan, turning carefully to brown evenly. Serve
immediately with the Sweet & Feisty Crème Fraîche.

# SALUMI CHIPS

12 slices salumi of your
  choice

**MAKES 12**

Preheat the oven to 180°C (350°F) Gas 4.

Lay the slices of salumi in a single layer on a baking
sheet. Bake in the preheated oven for 20–25 minutes
until crisp. Keep checking that they're not burning.
Remove from the oven and let cool.

Store in an airtight container in the fridge for up
to a week; a perfect snack to nibble on.

# TOMATO BACON GRATIN

1 tablespoon olive oil
2 bacon rashers/slices,
  finely chopped
1 shallot, finely chopped
25 g/½ cup fresh
  breadcrumbs
a pinch of dried oregano
4 tomatoes

10 g/2 tablespoons grated
  Parmesan cheese
salt and freshly ground
  black pepper, to season

*a shallow ovenproof casse-
role dish, oiled*

**SERVES 4**

Preheat the oven to 200°C (400°F) Gas 6.

Heat the oil in a small frying pan/skillet set over
medium heat. Add the bacon and shallot and fry
for 2–3 minutes, stirring often, until the shallot has
softened and the bacon is cooked. Remove from
the heat and stir in the breadcrumbs and oregano.

Slice the tomatoes into 1-cm/½-inch-thick slices.
Arrange in the prepared casserole dish, overlapping
slightly. Season with a little salt and pepper, bearing
in mind the saltiness of the bacon.

Spread the bacon mixture evenly over the tomato
slices, then sprinkle over the Parmesan. Bake in the
preheated oven for 20 minutes and serve hot from
the oven.

# 'SCOTCH EGGS'

12 quails' eggs
6 slices prosciutto, coppa
  or Serrano ham
sea salt and freshly ground
  black pepper, to season

**MAKES 12**

Hard-boil/hard-cook the quails' eggs
in a pan of boiling water for 5 minutes.
Drain and plunge the eggs into cold
water, then drain again and let cool.
Remove the shells, dry the eggs with
paper towels and then roll them in salt
and pepper.

Cut each slice of cured ham lengthways
down the middle (standard kitchen

scissors are easiest for doing this)
to make 12 half-slices in total.

Roll each quails' egg up inside
a half-slice of ham. You might need
to insert a cocktail stick/toothpick
through each canapé if the quails' eggs
are bigger, but they'll hold together
by themselves if they're small. Serve
immediately.

# CHEESE & CHUTNEY NIGHT

Nothing says 'mature, sophisticated get-together' like a selection of mature, sophisticated cheeses, beautifully combined with a fancy chutney or snazzy salad. Gather your most grown-up friends, then impress them with your cheeseboard, bursting with French Camembert, Italian burrata and whatever other creamy, crumbly, stinky delights you can find at your local fromagerie (or, you know, supermarket cheese section). Then pair each one with the perfect wine – because being such a connoisseur, you'd know what that'd be, right?

## SMALL PLATES & SIDES
Apple, Sage & Calvados Chutney
Fig Chutney
Blue Cheese & Walnut Bites

## BIGGER BITES
Sun-Blush Tomato, Orange & Burrata Salad
Trio of Honey-Baked Camembert

## SOMETHING SWEET
Fig & Honey Ricotta Cheesecake

## DRINKS
Cheesecake Martini

# APPLE, SAGE & CALVADOS CHUTNEY

6 apples, peeled, cored and diced
120 ml/½ cup Calvados or other apple liqueur
450 g/2¼ cups caster/granulated sugar
1 teaspoon dried sage

grated zest and juice of 1 lemon

*sterilized glass jars with airtight lids*

**MAKES 950 ML/1 QUART**

Place the apple pieces in a large pan with 710 ml/3 cups water. Bring to a boil over medium-high heat. Reduce the heat and simmer for about 45 minutes, stirring occasionally, until the apples are soft.

Place the cooked apples in a blender and purée. Return the purée to the pan and add the Calvados, sugar, sage and lemon zest and juice. Bring to a boil, then reduce the heat and simmer for about 40 minutes, stirring frequently. The paste should be thick and deep in colour.

Put the paste into sterilized glass jars, leaving a little space from the top. Carefully tap on the counter top to remove air pockets. Wipe the jars clean and screw on the lids. Keep in the fridge for up to 1 month.

# FIG CHUTNEY

25 g/2 tablespoons butter
1 red onion, finely diced
12 fresh figs, peeled and chopped
40 g/3 tablespoons soft/packed brown sugar
3 tablespoons red wine vinegar
a pinch of ground ginger

a handful of sultanas/golden raisins
juice of ¼ lemon

*a sterilized glass jar with an airtight lid*

**MAKES 1 JAR (ABOUT 200 G/7 OZ.)**

Melt the butter in a frying pan/skillet, then add the onion and fry over fairly high heat until it's soft and starting to brown. Stir in the figs and sugar, then add the vinegar, ginger and sultanas/golden raisins. Add the lemon juice and 3 tablespoons water. Reduce the heat to a low simmer and cook, uncovered, for 10–15 minutes until the mixture thickens, stirring now and then.

Remove from the heat and let cool, then transfer to a sterilized jar or a suitable airtight container and cover. Store in the fridge. It is best to make this chutney at least 24 hours before serving, to let the flavours mature.

Note: This chutney will keep (if sealed) for a couple of weeks in the fridge. You can also freeze it (in an airtight container). Just check the flavour after you thaw it, as it might need a little top-up of seasoning – perhaps a little more ground ginger or a squeeze of fresh lemon juice.

# BLUE CHEESE & WALNUT BITES

90 g/6 tablespoons butter, softened
130 g/4¹/₂ oz. strong blue cheese, such
    as Roquefort
200 g/1²/₃ cups plain/all-purpose flour
a pinch of salt
50 g/¹/₂ cup walnuts, chopped

*2 baking sheets lined with parchment paper*

**MAKES ABOUT 30**

Preheat the oven to 180°C (350°F) Gas 4.

Beat the butter and blue cheese together in
a mixing bowl until evenly mixed. Work in the flour
and salt and bring the mixture together to form a
smooth dough. Add the chopped walnuts and knead
very lightly until they have all been evenly combined.
Form the mixture into two long sausage shapes and
wrap each in clingfilm/plastic wrap. Refrigerate
for 30 minutes to firm up.

Unwrap the dough and cut into slices just under
1 cm/¹/₂ inch thick. Arrange on the prepared baking
sheets, leaving a little space for spreading between
each one. Bake in the oven for 10–12 minutes until
crisp and golden.

Let cool for 5 minutes before transferring to
a wire rack to cool completely. Store in an airtight
container for up to 5 days.

# SUN-BLUSH TOMATO, ORANGE & BURRATA SALAD

2 large oranges
24 sun-blush/semi-dried cherry tomato
 halves
2 burrata cheeses (or good-quality fresh
 mozzarella cheese)
extra virgin olive oil, for drizzling
freshly ground black pepper, to season
a handful of basil leaves, to garnish

**SERVES 4**

Peel the oranges, making sure to trim off all the white pith, and cut into thick, even slices.

Place the orange slices on a large serving dish, then scatter over the sun-blush/semi-dried tomato halves. Tear the burrata cheeses into chunks and layer on top of the orange slices.

Drizzle with extra virgin olive oil and season with pepper. Garnish with basil leaves and serve at once.

# TRIO OF HONEY-BAKED CAMEMBERT

3 x 250-g/8-oz. Camembert cheeses in boxes
 (Vacherin Mont d'Or works just as well)
3 tablespoons Calvados or brandy
3 tablespoons dark chestnut honey
1 fat garlic clove, sliced
3 sage leaves
3 rosemary sprigs
3 bay leaves

TO SERVE (OPTIONAL)
celery sticks
walnut bread
chilled French breakfast radishes

**SERVES ABOUT 15**

Preheat the oven to 200°C (400°F) Gas 6.

Unwrap the cheeses and return them to their boxes. Using a skewer, make six holes in each cheese. Mix the Calvados or brandy and honey together and spoon over the holes. Stud with the garlic and press the herbs onto each cheese. Bake for about 7 minutes.

Remove the boxes from the oven. Using sharp scissors, quickly make three cuts on the surface of each cheese, from the centre out, and gently open the 'petals' a little. Take the cheeses out of their boxes, put them on a plate and serve straight away.

# FIG & HONEY RICOTTA CHEESECAKE

150 g/5½ oz. digestive biscuits/graham crackers

50 g/3½ tablespoons butter, melted

750 g/3 cups ricotta

2 eggs

2 tablespoons honey

½ teaspoon orange flower water

40 g/⅓ cup plain/all-purpose flour

6 fresh figs, halved

20-cm/8-inch loose-based cake pan

SERVES 6

Preheat the oven to 180°C (350°F) Gas 3.

Using a rolling pin, crush the biscuits/crackers into fine crumbs.

In a large bowl, mix the crumbs with the melted butter. Next, press this mixture firmly and evenly into the cake pan to form a crust.

In a separate large bowl, mix together the ricotta and eggs. Stir in the honey, orange flower water and flour.

Spoon the ricotta mixture evenly across the biscuit crust. Now, press the halved figs, skinside down, into the ricotta mixture.

Bake the cheesecake in the preheated oven for 50 minutes to 1 hour until set. Remove the pan from the oven and cool, then cover and chill until serving.

The cheesecake will keep for a few days, covered, in the fridge.

# CHEESECAKE MARTINI

1 digestive biscuit/ graham cracker

10 ml/2 teaspoons sugar syrup

50 ml/2 fl. oz. vodka

12.5 ml/⅓ fl. oz. Chambord

12.5 ml/⅓ fl. oz. raspberry purée

12.5 ml/⅓ fl. oz. double/heavy cream

MAKES 1

Grind the biscuit/cracker into crumbs, add the sugar syrup, mix and pack into the bottom of a martini glass.

Put the remaining ingredients into a cocktail shaker, shake well and strain gently over the crumbs into the martini glass.

# AVOCADELICIOUS

Calling all avocado aficionados. Gone are the days when avocados were only associated with guacamole and face masks. Kick some hipster hass with these rich, goopy dishes, all using the mean, green superfood as their star ingredient – served with a healthy, 'good-fat' side of antioxidants. Before your guests arrive, tease them with some Instagram posts of what's waiting for them at yours. They'll soon be ripe for an avo injection! Because everything in moderation... except avocado.

### SMALL PLATES & SIDES

Avocado Miso Dip with Root Vegetable
Crisps & Dukkah Spice Mix

### BIGGER BITES

Peach & Avocado Panzanella
Everything Avocado Toast

### SOMETHING SWEET

Choco-Avo Mousse

### DRINKS

Avocado Margarita

# AVOCADO MISO DIP WITH ROOT VEGETABLE CRISPS & DUKKAH SPICE MIX

20 g/2½ tablespoons blanched hazelnuts
20 g/2½ tablespoons blanched almonds
2 tablespoons sesame seeds
1 tablespoon cumin seeds
1 tablespoon coriander seeds
1 tablespoon dried mint
120 g/4 oz. avocado flesh (prepared weight)
1 tablespoon brown miso paste
1 tablespoon freshly squeezed lemon juice
2 teaspoons tahini
2 teaspoons extra virgin olive oil, plus extra
   to serve
1 small garlic clove, crushed
sea salt

ROOT VEGETABLE CRISPS/CHIPS
2 medium beet(root)s
2 medium parsnips
olive oil, for roasting
sea salt

*a mandolin grater*
*2 baking sheets lined with parchment paper*

**SERVES 2**

You can buy a packet of root vegetable crisps/chips if you're pushed for time, but if you'd like to make your own, first preheat the oven to 200°C (400°F) Gas 6. Peel, top and tail the beet(root)s and the parsnips (or any other root vegetable), then using the mandolin grater, cut into paper-thin slices. Pat dry with paper towels. Place in a bowl and toss lightly with olive oil to give them a very thin coat – not too much otherwise they will be soggy rather than crisp. Toss with a little sea salt, then lay out one by one and not overlapping on the prepared baking sheets. Roast for 5–8 minutes, keeping a sharp eye on them, as they burn easily. Remove and let cool completely before moving them to a bowl.

Reduce the oven temperature to 180°C (350°F) Gas 4.

Roast the nuts and seeds on separate baking sheets, the hazelnuts for about 5 minutes and the almonds and sesame seeds for 8 minutes. Let cool.

Meanwhile, in a dry frying pan/skillet over medium heat, fry the cumin seeds and coriander seeds for 1–2 minutes until fragrant.

In a food processor, blitz the spices, roasted nuts and seeds, dried mint and ½ teaspoon sea salt until finely ground. Be careful not to blend for too long, though, as the nuts will begin to release oils and it will turn from a powder to a paste. Carefully spoon the mixture into a bowl and set aside.

Blitz the avocado in the food processor with the miso paste, lemon juice, tahini, olive oil and garlic until completely smooth. Taste and adjust the seasoning if necessary.

Serve the vegetable crisps/chips in a shallow serving bowl.

Scatter some of the dukkah onto the avocado miso dip and drizzle with oil. To eat, dunk the crisps/chips into the dip and then into the remaining dukkah, which will cling nicely onto the wet dip.

# PEACH & AVOCADO PANZANELLA

½ small red onion, very thinly sliced
½ tablespoon red wine vinegar
2 peaches, stoned/pitted and cut into
    2-cm/¾-inch wedges
olive oil, for brushing and drizzling
15 baby plum tomatoes, halved
1 avocado, peeled, stoned/pitted and
    chopped into bite-sized chunks
1 full-length slice sourdough bread
1 small garlic clove, halved
2 tablespoons extra virgin olive oil
1 bunch of basil, roughly chopped
1 teaspoon Thai red chilli/chili paste
freshly ground black pepper, to season

**SERVES 2**

Place the sliced red onion in a bowl with the red wine vinegar and a pinch of sea salt. Toss together and set aside to let the flavours infuse.

Place a ridged stove-top griddle/grill pan over a high heat. Lightly brush the peach wedges with just enough olive oil to coat them. Add the peaches to the pan and cook for a couple of minutes until charred on one side. Flip over and cook on the other side. Transfer to a plate while you prepare the other ingredients.

In a large mixing bowl, gently toss the tomato halves and avocado chunks together with the peaches in 1 tablespoon of the extra virgin olive oil and a good pinch of salt. Set aside.

Toast the sourdough bread until golden brown and crunchy on the outside. Rub the garlic clove over the hot bread, then drizzle some olive oil over the bread and let soak in.

Finely chop the leftover garlic and add it to the tomato mix, with the chopped basil and vinegar-infused red onion slices.

For the dressing, combine the Thai red chilli/chili paste with the remaining tablespoon of extra virgin olive oil in a small bowl. Add this to the salad bowl and then tear the bread into the salad in rough chunks. Gently combine everything until well mixed. Taste and season with black pepper and more sea salt if needed. Pile the panzanella onto a flat serving dish and serve.

# EVERYTHING AVOCADO TOAST

2 large (or 4 small) slices sourdough,
    whole grain or sprouted grain bread
1 avocado, peeled, stoned/pitted and
    roughly chopped
1 spring onion/scallion, finely sliced
Everything Bagel Spice Mix
    (see Note – the whole batch will keep
    for up to 6 months in an airtight jar)

**SERVES 2**

Toast the bread to your liking, then top with the avocado, dividing it evenly between each slice. Use a fork to mash the avocado, pressing it into the toast. Sprinkle with the sliced spring onion/scallion and finally with some of the Everything Bagel Spice Mix.

Note: For the Everything Bagel Spice Mix, toast 1 tablespoon sesame seeds in a dry frying pan/skillet over medium-low heat for about 5 minutes. Remove from heat to cool. Put 1 tablespoon each poppy seeds, dried garlic granules and onion powder and 2 teaspoons salt in an airtight jar and shake to combine.

# CHOCO-AVO MOUSSE

40 g/3 tablespoons
coconut oil
2 large ripe avocados,
peeled and stoned/
pitted
4 tablespoons/¼ cup
unsweetened cocoa
powder
4 tablespoon pure maple
syrup

1 teaspoons/¼ cup
pure vanilla extract
200 ml/¾ cup coconut
milk
100 g/½ cup coconut
palm sugar
2 rosemary sprigs, plus
a few leaves to serve
about 15 raspberries
sea salt

**SERVES 4**

Melt the coconut oil in a heatproof bowl over
a saucepan of simmering water.

Add the avocados, cocoa powder, maple syrup,
vanilla and a good pinch of sea salt to a food
processor and blitz for a few seconds. Add in the
melted coconut oil and blitz until completely
smooth. Remove to a bowl, cover and refrigerate
for at least 2 hours.

To make the caramel, place the coconut milk and
coconut palm sugar in a saucepan over medium-high
heat. Bring to a boil, stirring all the time, then reduce
the heat, add the rosemary and a pinch of sea salt
and simmer for 10 minutes, stirring on and off, until
you have a thick, viscous caramel.

When ready to serve, warm the caramel and then
spoon the set chocolate mousse in a misshapen
mound onto the centre of a cold bowl or plate.
Drizzle over the warm rosemary caramel, add a few
raspberries onto each dish and scatter over some
rosemary leaves and a very small pinch of sea salt
to serve.

# AVOCADO MARGARITA

½ teaspoon chilli/chili
powder
1 lime, cut into wedges,
plus extra to serve
2 ripe avocados, peeled
and stoned/pitted
450 g/3 cups ice
180 ml/¾ cup freshly

squeezed lime juice
1½ teaspoons agave nectar
250 ml/1 cup tequila
125 ml/½ cup Triple Sec
3 coriander/cilantro sprigs
(optional)
1 tablespoon sea salt

**MAKES 4–6**

Combine all the ingredients, except the salt,
in a blender and blend until icy and smooth.

Place the sea salt on a plate. Dampen the rims
of the glasses, then dip them in the salt. Pour in the
margaritas and serve with lime wedges on the side.

# VEGAN CELEBRATION

Enjoying the lentil things in life is what it's all about - the days when non-vegans would wrinkle their nose and ask, 'But HOW do you get your protein?', and assumed that vegans only survived on hummus, are long gone. Hurrah! Play your dinner party V-card just right by serving creative, taste bud-tickling dishes that say, 'No whey, Jose!' to blah and 'Yes peas!' to healthful, mouthwatering fare.

### SMALL PLATES & SIDES
Baked Tortilla Chips
Creamy Chipotle Dip
Garlic Yogurt Dip
Basic Avocado Dip

### BIGGER BITES
Jerusalem Artichokes
Buffalo Cauliflower & Chickpea Bowl

### SOMETHING SWEET
Aquafaba Pavlova with Fresh Fruit

### DRINKS
Peach Julep

Who's up for some (not-so-skinny) dipping? Leave your inhibitions at the door and dive into these divine dips. If you're holding your dinner party on March 23rd, you can congratulate yourself on tying this in with America's National Chip and Dip Day (yes, that's a thing!). If this date doesn't work for you, however, fret not... these recipes are so moreish that your guests will go dippy for them every day of the week and twice on Sunday. Pass the chips.

# BAKED TORTILLA CHIPS

3 x 15-cm/6-inch flour tortillas
½ tablespoon sunflower oil, plus extra for oiling
sea salt, for sprinkling

**MAKES 24**

Preheat the oven to 200°C (400°F) Gas 6. Brush the tortillas on one side with the oil. Cut each one into eight even-sized wedges with kitchen scissors. Arrange them oiled side up on an oiled baking sheet and sprinkle with salt. Bake for 5–7 minutes until browned and crisp. Let cool on a wire rack before serving.

# CREAMY CHIPOTLE DIP

75 g/⅓ cup tahini, mixed well
1 chipotle chili/chile in adobo sauce or ½ tablespoon chipotle chilli/chili paste
1 tablespoon adobo sauce from the pepper can (omit if using the paste)
1 tablespoon freshly squeezed lime juice
1 teaspoon maple syrup
½ teaspoon salt
1 garlic clove, peeled

**MAKES ABOUT 235 ML/1 CUP**

Place all the ingredients in a food processor and blend together with 75 ml/⅓ cup water until smooth. Add more water, if needed, to reach the desired consistency.

# GARLIC YOGURT DIP

215 g/scant 1 cup non-dairy yogurt
1 garlic clove, chopped or finely grated
1 tablespoon olive oil, plus extra to serve
¼ teaspoon salt
freshly ground black pepper, to season

**MAKES ABOUT 235 ML/1 CUP**

In a small bowl, stir together the dip ingredients with a fork.

To serve, drizzle with additional olive oil and freshly ground black pepper, if desired.

# BASIC AVOCADO DIP

1 avocado, peeled and stoned/pitted
freshly squeezed juice of ½ lemon or lime
a small handful of coriander/cilantro leaves
sea salt, to season

**MAKES ABOUT 175–235 ML/ ¾–1 CUP**

In a food processor or blender, place the avocado, lemon or lime juice, coriander/cilantro leaves and a good pinch of sea salt. Blend to a smooth purée.

Add water, a tablespoon at a time, and blend again until you reach the desired consistency – thick enough for a dip but thin enough to drizzle. Taste and add extra sea salt, if desired.

# JERUSALEM ARTICHOKES

4 shallots, peeled
6 garlic cloves, peeled
½ cauliflower, cut into
  florets
1–2 tablespoons olive oil
1 teaspoon freshly ground
  white pepper
1 kg/2¼ lbs. Jerusalem
  artichokes/sunchokes
425 ml/1¾ cups almond
  milk or other vegan
  milk, plus extra if
  needed
2 tablespoons freshly
  squeezed lemon juice
½ teaspoon mustard
  powder

1 teaspoon onion powder
1 teaspoon salt
1 slice brown or rye
  bread, blitzed to rough
  breadcrumbs
3 tablespoons panko
  breadcrumbs
1 tablespoon chopped
  marjoram or parsley
  (or ½ teaspoon dried)
2 tablespoons toasted
  hazelnuts, roughly
  chopped

**SERVES 4–6**

Preheat the oven to 220°C (425°F) Gas 7.

Lay the shallots, garlic cloves and cauliflower on a baking sheet and drizzle with half of the olive oil and then season with half of the pepper. Peel and slice the artichokes into 5-mm/¼-inch-thick discs. Lay them on another baking sheet, drizzle with the rest of the olive oil and season with the remaining pepper. Place both baking sheets in the preheated oven and roast for 30 minutes.

Transfer the roasted shallots, garlic and cauliflower, to a food processor or blender and add the almond milk, lemon juice, mustard powder, onion powder and salt. Blitz until very smooth. Layer the artichoke slices in a baking dish and pour over the sauce. Sprinkle over the breadcrumbs, herbs and hazelnuts. Bake in the oven for about 30 minutes until golden on top and bubbling.

Carrots, peas, cucumbers: all solid vegetables that have their place on our plates. But sometimes it's good to go kerrr-azy and try things a bit more exotic. Enter the Jerusalem artichoke, which – go figure! – isn't from Jerusalem and isn't an artichoke. Also known as a sunchoke, sunroot or earth apple, this root vegetable is a relative of the sunflower and, like the bright yellow bloom, will put a smile on your face.

# BUFFALO CAULIFLOWER & CHICKPEA BOWL

**TAHINI-RANCH DRESSING**
**(makes about 175 ml/³/₄ cup)**
50 g/3½ tablespoons
  tahini, mixed well
60 ml/¼ cup warm water
2 tablespoons finely
  chopped chives
1 tablespoon finely
  chopped parsley
1 teaspoon onion powder
1 teaspoon garlic powder
½ teaspoon dried dill
1 teaspoon maple syrup
juice of ½ lemon
½ teaspoon salt
a few grinds of black
  pepper, to season

**CAULIFLOWER**
1 small–medium head of
  cauliflower, chopped
  into florets
1 tablespoon olive oil
3 tablespoons hot sauce

salt, to season

**CHICKPEAS**
1 tablespoon avocado
  or olive oil
1 x 400-g/14-oz. can
  chickpeas, drained and
  rinsed
¼ teaspoon garlic powder
2 tablespoons hot sauce
salt, to season

**SALAD**
1 bunch of cavolo nero/
  Tuscan kale, stems
  removed and shredded
1–2 tablespoons Tahini-
  Ranch Dressing (see
  above left), plus extra
  to serve
1 large carrot, peeled into
  ribbons
½ small red onion, thinly
  sliced into half-moons

**SERVES 2–4**

Preheat the oven to 220°C (425°F) Gas 7.

First make the Tahini-Ranch Dressing. In a small bowl, beat together all the ingredients until well combined. Or, purée everything in a small food processor. Add a touch more water, if needed, to thin to your desired consistency. Set aside.

Prepare the cauliflower by adding it to a large bowl with the oil and 1 tablespoon of the hot sauce. Season with salt and mix together until the cauliflower is well coated. Spread out on a baking sheet and roast in the preheated oven for 20 minutes. Take out and toss with the remaining 2 tablespoons of hot sauce. Return to the oven for 5–10 minutes until the cauliflower is lightly browned at the edges.

To make the chickpeas, heat the oil in a large frying pan/skillet over medium-high heat. Then add the chickpeas, garlic powder and salt to season. Cook for 3 minutes, tossing regularly. Stir in 1 tablespoon of the hot sauce and cook, stirring, for 2–3 minutes, until the chickpeas are starting to brown. Remove from the heat and stir in the remaining tablespoon of hot sauce.

Combine the cavolo nero/Tuscan kale with the Tahini-Ranch Dressing in a large bowl. Massage into the cavolo nero/Tuscan kale for 2 minutes until it begins to soften a little. Toss in the carrot and red onion and mix until everything is well coated in the dressing. Divide the salad into bowls and top with the cauliflower, chickpeas and extra Tahini-Ranch Dressing.

# AQUAFABA PAVLOVA WITH FRESH FRUIT

150 g/3/4 cup caster/superfine sugar
2 tablespoons arrowroot powder
   or cornflour/cornstarch
a pinch of salt
liquid from 1 x 400-g/14-oz. can of
   no-added-salt (low-sodium) organic
   chickpeas, chilled in the fridge overnight
1 teaspoon white vinegar
1 teaspoon vanilla extract

TO SERVE
1 x 400-g/14-oz. can full-fat coconut milk,
   cooled in the fridge overnight
2 teaspoons maple syrup
1/2 teaspoon vanilla extract
220 g/1/2 lb. mixed prepared fresh fruit
icing/confectioners' sugar for dusting
   (optional)

a large baking sheet lined with
   parchment paper

SERVES 6–8

Preheat the oven to 150°C (300°F) Gas 2.

Place a large mixing bowl in the freezer for a few minutes to make it extra cold. In another bowl, combine the sugar, arrowroot (or cornflour/cornstarch) and salt.

In the large chilled bowl, put the chilled aquafaba liquid and vinegar and beat with an electric hand mixer or in a stand mixer at medium speed for about 2–4 minutes until soft peaks begin to form, scraping down the sides of the bowl. While still mixing, start adding the sugar mixture, one spoonful at a time. When all the sugar has been added, beat for about 3–6 minutes until stiff, glossy peaks form. Add the vanilla and beat for another 10 seconds.

Tip the mixture onto the prepared baking sheet and form into a 20-cm/8-inch-wide circle using a rubber spatula. Leave space around the edges, as it will spread a bit. Put in the oven and immediately lower the heat to 120°C (250°F) Gas 1/2. Bake for 1 1/2–2 hours until the outer shell is hardened when you tap it.

Meanwhile scoop out the hardened coconut cream from the top of the can (reserving the coconut water for something else) and put the cream in the chilled mixing bowl. Whip for 1–2 minutes using an electric hand mixer until light and smooth. Add the maple syrup and vanilla and whip again to combine for about 1 minute more. Set aside.

Turn off the oven and let the pavlova cool completely inside the closed oven. When ready to serve, top with the coconut whipped cream, fruit and icing/confectioners' sugar, if using.

# PEACH JULEP

5 mint leaves
20 ml/2/3 fl. oz. bourbon
25 ml/1 fl. oz. peach juice
5 ml/1 teaspoon peach schnapps
a handful of ice cubes
well-chilled Champagne or other dry
   sparkling wine, to top
peach slice, to garnish

MAKES 1

Muddle the mint leaves with the bourbon in a cocktail shaker. Add the peach juice and peach schnapps with a handful of ice cubes and shake well.

Strain into a chilled Champagne coupe, garnish with a peach slice and serve.

# FAMILY COOK-IN

You may not be able to choose your family, but you can choose what
you serve them. Gather the generations together and tuck into this feed-me
feast that brings the cook-out indoors, so can be enjoyed whatever the
weather. Cluster around your dining table and watch as your clan gets
stuck into your homemade burgers with a twist, crowd-pleasing coleslaw
and chicken wings to make your dad proud. An evening a-kin to perfection.

## SMALL PLATES & SIDES

Celeriac Remoulade

Apple Slaw

Sweet Potato Fries

## BIGGER BITES

Not Your Dad's BBQ Wings

Chorizo & Bean Burger

## DRINKS

Homemade Root Beer Float

Homemade Cola

# NOT YOUR DAD'S BBQ WINGS

1 small onion, finely chopped
250 ml/1 cup teriyaki sauce
250 ml/1 cup oyster sauce
120 ml/½ cup soy sauce
140 ml/scant ⅔ cup tomato ketchup
4 tablespoons/¼ cup garlic powder
120 ml/⅓ cup gin
2 teaspoons cayenne pepper
1 teaspoon mustard powder
200 g/1 cup soft/packed brown sugar
1.8 kg/4 lbs. chicken wings,
    halved at the joints, tips removed
vegetable oil, for oiling
80 g/¼ cup honey
blue cheese dip, to serve

**SERVES 4**

In a large bowl, mix together the onion, teriyaki sauce, oyster sauce, soy sauce, ketchup, garlic powder, gin, cayenne pepper, mustard powder and brown sugar. Place the chicken wings in the bowl, cover and marinate in the fridge for 8 hours or overnight.

Preheat the grill/broiler to low.

Lightly oil the wire rack of the grill/broiler. Arrange the chicken on the rack, discarding the marinade. Grill/broil the chicken wings on one side for 20 minutes, then turn and brush with the honey. Continue grilling/broiling for 25 minutes or until cooked through and the juices run clear when the thickest part is pierced to the bone. These wings are good served with a blue cheese dip.

# CELERIAC REMOULADE

½ celeriac/celery root,
    peeled and grated/
    shredded
juice of ½ lemon
    (see Note)
1 teaspoon mustard (Dijon
    or wholegrain are best)

a big pinch of chopped
    parsley
a pinch of fennel seeds
a pinch of sea salt

**SERVES 4**

Combine all the ingredients in a bowl, mixing them together well, and chill in the fridge, covered, for at least 1 hour before serving so that the flavours can be absorbed.

Note: Add the juice of ½ lemon first and then taste and add a little more, if you like.

# APPLE SLAW

1 tablespoon apple cider
    vinegar
2 tablespoons mayonnaise
¼ white cabbage, cored
    and shredded
1 carrot, grated/shredded
4–5 spring onions/
    scallions, finely chopped
a big pinch of chopped
    parsley

2 eating/dessert apples,
    cored and coarsely
    grated/shredded
    (leave the peel on)
sea salt and freshly ground
    black pepper, to season

**SERVES 2–3**

Pop all the ingredients into a bowl and mix well. Be sure to taste the slaw and then adjust the seasoning and add more of anything to suit your taste. Cover and refrigerate until you are ready to serve.

Try to make this at least 1 hour before serving so that you can chill it really well and let the flavours mingle.

# CHORIZO & BEAN BURGER

**BURGERS**
400 g/14 oz. lean minced/
  ground beef
125 g/4½ oz. chorizo, finely
  diced
80 g/scant ½ cup canned
  red kidney beans
  (drained weight), rinsed,
  drained and crushed
60 g/1 cup fresh
  breadcrumbs
4 teaspoons tomato
  purée/paste

1 teaspoon chopped
  parsley
sea salt and freshly ground
  black pepper, to season

**TO SERVE**
4 crusty bread rolls or
  toasted English muffins,
  halved
salad leaves/greens
red onion chutney, if liked

**SERVES 4 (MAKES 4
CHUNKY 175-G/6-OZ.
BURGERS)**

Put all the burger ingredients in a large bowl and mix together really well with your hands. Divide the mixture into four and then shape each portion into a burger.

To cook the burgers, fry them in a frying pan/skillet over medium heat for 12–15 minutes, turning a few times, until cooked through. Alternatively, pop them on the rack in a grill/broiler pan and cook under a preheated hot grill/broiler for 6 minutes on each side until cooked through.

Serve the hot burgers in the bread rolls or toasted English muffins with some salad leaves/greens and red onion chutney, if liked.

# SWEET POTATO FRIES

3 large sweet potatoes,
  scrubbed
2 tablespoons cornflour/
  cornstarch
vegetable oil, for deep-
  frying

sea salt flakes, for
  sprinkling

**SERVES 4 AS A SIDE**

Cut the sweet potatoes into thin pieces (about 1.5 cm/ ⅝ inch long), rinse and pat dry. Make up a batter with the cornflour/cornstarch and 2 tablespoons water in a shallow bowl. You will need to stir the batter in between coatings; it is also best made in small batches, so keep increasing as needed.

Fill a large saucepan one-third full with the oil or, if using a deep-fat fryer, follow the manufacturer's instructions. Heat the oil to 190°C (375°F) or until a cube of bread browns in 30 seconds.

Working in small batches, dip a handful of potatoes in the cornflour/cornstarch batter, then place in a frying basket and carefully lower into the oil. Fry for 1–2 minutes. Remove and drain on paper towels. Repeat until all of the potatoes have been fried. Just before serving, skim any debris off the top of the cooking oil and reheat to the same temperature.

Coat and fry as before, working in batches, but only cook until crisp and golden. Remove and drain on paper towels. Repeat until all of the potatoes have been fried. Sprinkle with salt flakes and serve.

Remember when you were a kid and you scraped your knee, you'd be given a hug, a get-better kiss and a cola or root beer float? Take a sip down memory lane and relive those simple days with these syrupy drinks served with a side of nostalgia. The fact that they're homemade - mixed with lashings of unconditional love - makes them all the more sweet.

## HOMEMADE COLA

400 g/2 cups white sugar
2 tablespoons soft/packed dark brown sugar
grated zest of 1 very large or 2 small-medium oranges
grated zest of 1 lime
grated zest of 1 lemon
2 teaspoons coriander seeds, crushed in a pestle and mortar

1½ teaspoons dried lavender
4 star anise
1 vanilla pod/bean, split
1 cinnamon stick
1 teaspoon finely chopped fresh root ginger
¼ teaspoon citric acid
soda water/club soda, to serve

**MAKES 4–6**

Place all the ingredients in a medium saucepan with 450 ml/2 cups water. Over medium heat, boil for 20 minutes, then remove from the heat and set the pan in a large bowl of ice.

To serve, dilute 1–2 tablespoons of the syrup with 225 ml/1 cup soda water/club soda.

## HOMEMADE ROOT BEER FLOAT

115 g/1 cup cut and sifted sassafras root bark
1 small bunch of mint leaves
grated zest of 1 lime
1 vanilla pod/bean, split and seeds scraped out
1 cinnamon stick

a pinch of ground coriander
a pinch of ground allspice
200 g/1 cup white sugar
85 g/¼ cup molasses
soda water/club soda, to serve

**MAKES 4–6**

Put the sassafras root bark and mint in a large saucepan. Add the lime zest, vanilla (seeds and pod/bean), cinnamon, coriander and allspice. Add 700 ml/3 cups water. Bring to a boil, then reduce the heat and simmer for 15–20 minutes until the mixture reduces by a third.

Strain through a fine-mesh sieve/strainer into a large jug/pitcher. While still warm, add the sugar and molasses and stir until dissolved.

To serve, dilute 1–2 tablespoons of the syrup with 225 ml/1 cup soda water/club soda.

# A NIGHT IN AT THE MOVIES

Nothing beats a fun night of flicks and food with friends. Roll out the red carpet for fellow movie buffs as you invite them over to feast on your Oscar-worthy spread, while tucking into whatever movie you play. Whether you go for action, adventure, comedy, horror, sci-fi or a tear-jerker, one thing's for sure: the food you serve will leave your guests hungry for more. So then perhaps play the sequel. Ready? Lights... Spatula... Action!

### SMALL PLATES & SIDES

Classic Fries
Chilli & Lime Garlic Mayo
Wild Garlic Dough Balls
Chilli Popcorn

### BIGGER BITES

Fried Corn Tortillas

### SOMETHING SWEET

Salted Caramel Popcorn

# CLASSIC FRIES

3–4 large floury potatoes,
    all roughly the same size
vegetable or sunflower oil,
    for deep-frying
sea salt flakes, for
    sprinkling

Chilli & Lime Garlic Mayo
    (see recipe, right),
    to serve

SERVES 4 AS A SIDE

Peel the potatoes and trim on all sides to get a block. Cut the block into slices about 1-cm/¹/₂-inch thick, then cut the slices again to get chips/fries.

Put the potatoes into a bowl of iced water for at least 5 minutes, to remove excess starch and prevent sticking when frying.

Fill a large saucepan one-third full with the oil or, if using a deep-fat fryer, follow the manufacturer's instructions. Heat the oil to 190°C (375°F) or until a cube of bread browns in 30 seconds.

Drain the potatoes and dry very well. Working in batches, fry about a handful of potatoes at a time. Place the potatoes in a frying basket (or use a slotted metal spoon) and lower into the hot oil carefully. Fry for 4 minutes. Remove and drain on paper towels. Repeat until all of the potatoes have been fried.

Just before serving, skim any debris off the top of the cooking oil and reheat to the same temperature. Fry as before, working in batches, but only cook until crisp and golden, for about 2 minutes. Remove and drain on paper towels. Repeat until all of the potatoes have been fried.

Sprinkle with the sea salt flakes and serve with the Chilli & Lime Garlic Mayo, or other dip of your liking.

# CHILLI & LIME GARLIC MAYO

250 g/generous 1 cup
    mayonnaise
2 garlic cloves, crushed
¹/₂ red chilli/chile, seeded
    and finely chopped

grated zest and juice
    of 1 lime

MAKES 250 G/
GENEROUS 1 CUP

Combine all the ingredients in a bowl and mix well. Let stand at least 30 minutes before serving.

# WILD GARLIC DOUGH BALLS

500 g/3³/₄ cups strong
    white/bread flour, plus
    extra for dusting
1 teaspoon fast-action
    dried/rapid-rise dry
    yeast
1¹/₂ teaspoons salt
1¹/₂ teaspoons sugar
300 ml/1¹/₄ cups hand-hot
    water

2 tablespoons olive oil,
    plus extra for oiling
75 g/5 tablespoons butter,
    softened
25 g/1 oz. wild garlic
    leaves/ramps, rinsed
    well and finely
    chopped

MAKES 24

For the dough, mix together the flour, yeast, salt and sugar in a mixing bowl. Gradually add the water and olive oil, bringing the mixture together to a sticky dough. Place on a lightly floured surface and knead until the dough is smooth and elastic. Place in a clean, oiled bowl, cover with a damp tea/kitchen towel and set aside in a warm place to rise for 1 hour until doubled.

Preheat the oven to 220°C (425°F) Gas 7.

Mix together the butter and wild garlic/ramps, and gently heat in a pan until just melted.

Divide the dough into 24 even-sized rounded balls. Place them on two oiled baking sheets, spaced apart. Brush each dough ball generously with the melted wild garlic/ramps butter and bake for 15–20 minutes in the oven until golden brown. Serve at once.

# FRIED CORN TORTILLAS

vegetable oil, for frying
10 corn tortillas, cut into
   8 wedges
2 tomatoes
5 dried chiles de árbol
   (or other hot dried red
   chillies/chiles), seeded
   and stems removed
1 teaspoon paprika
½ onion, finely chopped

2 eggs, beaten
a pinch of sea salt
100 g/scant 1 cup grated/
   shredded cheddar
   cheese
Mexican-Style Beans,
   to serve (optional,
   see page 14)

**SERVES 4**

Pour some vegetable oil into a deep saucepan until it comes 2 cm/³/₄ inch up the side of the pan. Set over medium heat and heat until the oil is very hot but not smoking.

Carefully drop the tortilla wedges into the oil, in batches of 10, and fry for about 30 seconds, turning the chips gently and often with tongs to prevent them from burning.

Using the tongs or a slotted spoon, remove the chips from the pan and let drain on paper towels. Repeat the process until all the chips have been fried. Reserve the oil.

Place 500 ml/2 cups water, the tomatoes and chillies/chiles in a saucepan and boil for 5 minutes.

Let cool for 10 minutes, then transfer all of it to a food processor with the paprika and whizz for 2 minutes or until smooth. Set aside.

Take 1 tablespoon of the reserved cooking oil and put in a large saucepan over medium heat.

Add the tortilla chips and onion to the pan, then add the eggs. Using a large spoon, very gently stir the mixture for 1 minute until the egg is cooked, but be careful not to break the fried tortilla chips.

Add the blended sauce, as well as the salt, and cook for 3–5 minutes or until the sauce is heated through – do not overcook it otherwise the tortillas will turn soggy. They need to be mixed well with the sauce but still retain a little of their crunchiness.

Preheat the grill/broiler to medium.

Transfer the fried corn tortillas to an ovenproof dish and sprinkle the cheese over the top. Grill/broil for 1–2 minutes to melt the cheese. Serve with Mexican-Style Beans, if you like.

# CHILLI POPCORN

1–2 tablespoons sunflower or vegetable oil
90 g/¹/₂ cup popcorn kernels
1 teaspoon salt
1–3 small dried bird's eye chillies/chiles
2 teaspoons caster/superfine sugar
juice of 1 lime

**MAKES 1 LARGE BOWL**

Heat the oil in a large lidded saucepan with a few popcorn kernels in the pan. When you hear the kernels pop, carefully tip in the rest of the kernels. Shake the pan over the heat until the popping stops. Take care when lifting the lid, as any unpopped kernels may still pop from the heat of the pan. Tip the popcorn into a bowl, removing any unpopped kernels as you go.

Grind the salt, chillies/chiles and sugar in a mortar and pestle until the chillies/chiles are completely broken down to a fine dust. Sprinkle the chilli/chile mix over the popcorn and squeeze over a little lime juice to bring out the flavour. Stir well so that the popcorn is evenly coated and serve warm or cold.

# SALTED CARAMEL POPCORN

1–2 tablespoons sunflower or vegetable oil
90 g/¹/₂ cup popcorn kernels for the
    caramel sauce
75 g/¹/₃ cup caster/superfine sugar
40 g/3 tablespoons butter
¹/₄ teaspoon sea salt
90 ml/¹/₃ cup double/heavy cream

TO SERVE
100 g/3¹/₂ oz. vanilla fudge, chopped
    into small cubes
40 g/1 cup mini mini marshmallows
    (see Note)

**MAKES 1 BOWL**

Heat the oil in a large lidded saucepan with a few popcorn kernels in the pan. When you hear the kernels pop, carefully tip in the rest of the kernels. Shake the pan over the heat until the popping stops. Take care when lifting the lid, as any unpopped kernels may still pop from the heat of the pan. Tip the popcorn into a bowl, removing any unpopped kernels as you go.

For the caramel sauce, put the sugar and butter in a small saucepan over gentle heat. Simmer until the butter has melted, the sugar has caramelized and you have a thick golden caramel sauce. Add the salt and stir again, taking care that the caramel does not burn. Add the cream gradually and heat, stirring all the time, until the sauce is thick and sticky. Pass through a sieve/strainer to remove any crystallized sugar pieces.

Pour the caramel over the popcorn and stir well so that each kernel is evenly coated. Set aside to cool for about 5 minutes. Sprinkle over the fudge and marshmallows and stir through. This popcorn can be served warm or cold.

Note: Mini mini marshmallows are available in supermarkets – they are the tiniest marshmallows you can imagine. If you cannot find them, you can substitute the slightly larger mini marshmallows or chop large marshmallows into small pieces using scissors.

# BRING-THE-PARTY-HOME KEBABS & SHOTS

After a few drinks on a night out, it's all-too easy to relent to the after-midnight munchies and shovel gawd-knows-what into your mouth. Forget that! Instead, stay in and savour the flavour of some more refined fare. How do lamb on a stick, skewered halloumi and skinny fries grab you? And you'll still be able to let your hair down with the libations in this chapter, but there's less chance of losing a shoe on your way home.

## SMALL PLATES & SIDES

Matchstick Fries

## BIGGER BITES

Lamb Koftes with Tahini Yogurt Dip
Halloumi & Mushroom Kebabs
Mini Kebabs with Flatbreads, Lemon & Parsley

## DRINKS

Tequila Slammer
B-52

# LAMB KOFTES
# WITH TAHINI YOGURT DIP

1 kg/1¼ lbs. minced/
    ground lamb
1½ teaspoons ground
    cumin
1½ teaspoons smoked
    sweet paprika
1 teaspoon ground allspice
1 teaspoon chilli/chili
    powder
150 g/1 cup (about 1 medium)
    finely diced red onion
25 g/½ cup finely chopped
    flat-leaf parsley
40 g/1 cup finely chopped
    coriander/cilantro, plus
    extra to serve
grated zest and juice of
    1 lemon, plus wedges
    to serve
3 UK large/US extra-large
    eggs

1 teaspoon sea salt
60 ml/¼ cup sunflower oil,
    for frying

**TAHINI YOGURT DIP**
250 ml/1 cup natural/plain
    Greek yogurt
2 tablespoons tahini paste
2 tablespoons freshly
    squeezed lemon juice
10 g/¼ cup finely chopped
    mint
¼ cucumber, grated
1 garlic clove, crushed
sea salt, to season

*30 x 15-cm/6-inch wooden
    skewers, soaked in water
    for at least 30 minutes*

**MAKES 30 SKEWERS
AND SERVES 10–15**

To make the koftes, place all of the ingredients except
the oil in a large mixing bowl and mix everything
together using your hands.

Shape the kofte mixture around the soaked skewers
(about 45–50 g/1½–2 oz. per skewer) in a sausage
shape and press the meat mixture firmly together.
Transfer to a baking sheet, cover with clingfilm/plastic
wrap and set in the fridge for at least 2 hours, or
preferably overnight, to firm up.

Preheat the oven to 180°C (350°F) Gas 4.

Heat the sunflower oil in a large frying pan/skillet over
medium-high heat. Add the koftes in batches and cook
for about 4 minutes, turning them until golden brown
all over. Transfer to a clean baking sheet while you
cook the remaining koftes in the same way as the
other. If necessary, add more oil to the pan each time.

When all the koftes have been fried, place them in the

preheated oven for 5 minutes to cook through.

To make the Tahini Yogurt Dip, mix all the ingredients
together and season with sea salt to taste.

Serve the koftes on a platter scattered with chopped
coriander/cilantro, lemon wedges and the Tahini
Yogurt Dip on the side.

# HALLOUMI &
# MUSHROOM KEBABS

250 g/½ lb. halloumi
    cheese, cut into 16
    even-sized pieces
16 even-sized button
    mushrooms, stems
    trimmed
12 cherry tomatoes
2 tablespoons olive oil
1 tablespoon chopped
    parsley leaves

8 bay leaves, stems
    trimmed, halved
8 thin lemon slices
salt and freshly ground
    black pepper, to season

*8 metal skewers*

**SERVES 4**

Preheat the grill/broiler.

In a large bowl, toss together the halloumi cheese,
button mushrooms, cherry tomatoes, olive oil
and parsley. Season with salt and pepper, bearing
in mind the natural saltiness of the halloumi.

Thread the cheese, mushrooms, cherry tomatoes,
bay leaves and lemon slices onto the 8 skewers.

Grill/broil the halloumi skewers for 5 minutes,
turning over halfway through, until the halloumi
is golden brown. Serve at once.

# MINI KEBABS WITH FLATBREADS, LEMON & PARSLEY

2 onions, peeled
½ tablespoon salt
2 garlic cloves, crushed
2 teaspoons cumin seeds, crushed
900 g/2 lbs. lean lamb, trimmed and cut
    into small bite-sized pieces

**FLATBREADS**
225 g/1²/₃ cups strong white/bread flour,
    plus extra for dusting
50 g/6 tablespoons wholemeal/whole-
    wheat flour
1 teaspoon salt
200 ml/³/₄ cup plus 2 tablespoons
    lukewarm water
1–2 tablespoons samna butter or
    1–2 tablespoons olive oil with a knob/pat
    of butter

**TO SERVE**
1 large red onion, halved lengthways,
    cut in half again crossways and sliced
    with the grain
1 large bunch of flat-leaf parsley, roughly
    chopped
2–3 lemons, halved

*a charcoal barbecue*
*wooden skewers, soaked in water for*
    *at least 30 minutes, or metal skewers*

**SERVES 4–6**

First, grate the onions onto a plate. Sprinkle the salt over the top and let the onions weep for about 15 minutes. Place a sieve/strainer over a bowl. Tip the weeping onion into the sieve/strainer, pressing it down with the back of a wooden spoon to extract the juice. Discard the onion that is left in the sieve/strainer. Mix the onion juice with the garlic and cumin seeds and toss in the lamb. Cover and let the lamb marinate in the fridge for 3–4 hours.

Meanwhile, prepare the dough for the flatbreads. Sift the flours with the salt into a bowl. Make a well in the centre and add the water gradually, drawing the flour in from the sides. Using your hands, knead the dough until firm and springy – if the dough is at all sticky, add more flour. Divide the dough into roughly 12 pieces and knead each one into a ball. Place the balls on a floured surface and cover with a damp tea/kitchen towel. Let rest for approximately 30 minutes.

Prepare your charcoal barbeque/grill. Just before cooking, roll out each ball of dough into wide, thin circles, keeping them dusted with flour so that they don't stick together, and cover them with a clean, damp tea/kitchen towel to prevent them from drying out. Quickly thread the meat onto skewers and place them over the hot charcoal for 2–3 minutes each side.

At the same time, heat a griddle or flat pan at one end of the charcoal barbeque/grill, or over a separate flame, and melt most of the samna (or olive oil and butter) in a small pot. Brush the hot griddle or flat pan with a little of the remaining samna (or olive oil and butter) and cook the flatbreads for about 15 seconds each side, flipping them over as soon as they begin to brown and buckle and continue brushing them with a little samna (or olive oil and butter). Pile them up on a plate and keep warm.

When the kebabs/kabobs are cooked, slide the meat off the skewers onto the flatbreads. Scatter some onion and parsley over each pile and squeeze the juice from the lemon halves over the top. Wrap the flatbreads into packages and eat with your hands.

# MATCHSTICK FRIES

2 large floury potatoes, roughly
   the same size
vegetable or sunflower oil, for frying
cornflour/cornstarch, for coating

**SICHUAN PEPPER SALT**
1 tablespoon Sichuan peppercorns
2 tablespoons coarse rock salt

**SERVES 4 AS A SIDE**

For the Sichuan Pepper Salt, heat the peppercorns
in a small frying pan/skillet until hot. Transfer to
a plate to cool. Combine with the salt and grind with
a pestle and mortar. Set aside.

Peel the potatoes and trim on all sides to get a block.
Cut the block into thin slices, then cut the slices
thinly into matchsticks. Put the potatoes into a bowl
of iced water for at least 5 minutes, to remove excess
starch and prevent sticking when frying. Put the
cornflour/cornstarch in a shallow bowl.

Fill a large saucepan one-third full with the oil and
heat the oil to 190°C (375°F) or until a cube of bread
browns in 30 seconds.

Drain the potatoes and pat dry, then toss to coat
lightly with the cornflour/cornstarch. Put in a sieve/
strainer to shake off any excess cornflour/cornstarch.

Working in batches, fry about a handful of potatoes
at a time. Place the potatoes in a frying basket and
lower into the hot oil carefully. Fry for about
5 minutes. Remove and drain on paper towels. Repeat
until all of the potatoes have been fried. Sprinkle
with the Sichuan Pepper Salt and serve.

# TEQUILA SLAMMER

60 ml/2 fl. oz. gold tequila
60 ml/2 fl. oz. Champagne (chilled)

**MAKES 1**

Pour both the tequila and the chilled champagne into
a highball glass with a sturdy base. Hold a napkin
over the glass (sealing the liquid inside), sharply slam
the glass down on a stable surface, and drink in one
go while it's fizzing.

# B-52

15 ml/½ fl. oz. Kahlúa
15 ml/½ fl. oz. Baileys
15 ml/½ fl. oz. Grand Marnier

**MAKES 1**

Layer each ingredient on top of each other over
a barspoon in a shot glass.

# SUPER BOWL CHICKEN WINGS FESTIVAL

Feast on (American) football and fabulous food as you host a Super Bowl home game. The crowd will go wild for your quarterback snacks, champion chomps and cocktails with a kick. Your chicken wings alone will score serious points in the taste department, while your guests will be huddled over your boozy baked beans until somebody calls a timeout to move onto your warm, wonderful waffles topped with a fried game hen. Touchdown!

### SMALL PLATES & SIDES

Bourbon Baked Beans

Crispy Pickled Vegetables

### BIGGER BITES

Spicy Grilled Orange-Honey Mustard Wings

Thai Peanut Wings

Fried Game Hen & Cornmeal Waffles

### DRINKS

Beer Margarita

Homemade Lemon-Lime Soda

# SPICY GRILLED ORANGE-HONEY MUSTARD WINGS

125 g/¹⁄₂ cup Dijon mustard
60 g/3 tablespoons honey
3 tablespoons mayonnaise
2 teaspoons steak sauce or
    Worcestershire sauce
grated zest of 1 orange
1.8 kg/4 lbs. chicken wings, halved
    at the joints, tips removed
vegetable oil, for oiling
coleslaw and mini corn on the cobs
    (or Elotes, see page 17), to serve

**SERVES 4–6**

Preheat the grill/broiler to medium.

Mix the mustard, honey, mayonnaise, steak or Worcestershire sauce and orange zest together in a small bowl. Set aside a small amount of the honey–mustard sauce for basting, and dip the chicken into the remaining sauce to coat.

Lightly oil the grill/broiler rack and grill/broil the chicken for about 20–25 minutes, turning occasionally, or until the chicken is cooked through and the juices run clear when the thickest part is pierced to the bone. Baste occasionally with the reserved sauce during the last 10 minutes.

Serve with coleslaw and mini corn on the cob (or Elotes).

# THAI PEANUT WINGS

4 garlic cloves, finely chopped
225 g/1 cup smooth peanut butter
120 ml/¹⁄₂ cup freshly squeezed lemon juice
1 tablespoon dried chilli/hot red
    pepper flakes
1¹⁄₂ tablespoons ground cumin
sea salt flakes, to season
1.8 kg/4 lbs. chicken wings, halved at the
    joints, tips removed
chopped flat-leaf parsley, to garnish
cucumber wedges, to serve

**SERVES 4–6**

Beat together the garlic, peanut butter, lemon juice, dried chilli/hot red pepper flakes and ground cumin with 250 ml/1 cup warm water; season with salt.

Toss the chicken wings with 225 g/1 cup of the sauce, cover and marinate in the fridge overnight or for at least 2 hours.

Preheat the grill/broiler and grill/broil the chicken for about 20–25 minutes, turning occasionally, until cooked through, lightly charred and the juices run clear when the thickest part is pierced to the bone.

Serve the wings with the remaining sauce, topped with chopped parsley and accompanied by cucumber wedges.

# BOURBON BAKED BEANS

450 g/1 lb. bacon, cut into 2.5-cm/1-inch
   pieces
1 onion, chopped
3 x 440-g/16-oz. cans baked beans
1 x 440-g/16-oz. can red kidney beans,
   drained
2 tablespoons dark molasses or treacle
2 tablespoons soft/packed dark
   brown sugar
80 ml/⅓ cup bourbon
120 ml/½ cup chilli/chili sauce
1 teaspoon mustard powder
1 teaspoon ground cinnamon

**SERVES 6–8**

Preheat the oven to 180°C (350°F) Gas 4.

Cook the bacon on a baking sheet in the oven or in
a frying pan/skillet on the hob/stovetop until crisp.
Drain and set aside, saving the bacon drippings.

Sauté the onion in the bacon drippings until it
is translucent.

In a large bowl, mix together the onion, baked beans,
kidney beans, molasses, sugar, bourbon, chilli/chili
sauce, mustard and cinnamon. Add the bacon and
fold in gently.

Pour the mixture into a large pot or casserole
dish. Cover with a lid or with foil. Bake the beans
for 40 minutes, then let stand for 10–15 minutes
before serving.

# CRISPY PICKLED VEGETABLES

450 g/1 lb. pickling cucumbers,
   sliced into thin wedges
450 g/1 lb. baby carrots, halved lengthways
1 fennel bulb, cored and cut into
   5 x 1-cm/2 x ½-inch matchsticks
1 red (bell) pepper, seeded and cut into
   5 x 1-cm/2 x ½-inch matchsticks
450 g/1 lb. green or pole beans, cut into
   5-cm/2-inch lengths
450 g/1 lb. celery, cut into
   5 x 1-cm/2 x ½-inch matchsticks
1 chilli/chile of your choice, cut into thin
   strips (optional, for heat)
700 ml/3 cups apple cider vinegar
120 ml/½ cup white wine vinegar
150 g/¾ cup white sugar
1 tablespoon sea salt flakes
1 teaspoon coriander seeds
1½ teaspoons black peppercorns
1 tablespoon fresh root ginger cut
   into matchsticks
1 bay leaf
9 garlic cloves, crushed

*a muslin/cheesecloth*
*large sterilized Mason/Kilner jars (optional)*

**Makes 2–3 jars**

In the words of star quarterback
Tom Brady, 'I could talk food all
day. I love good food.' And, boy,
are these pickled veg packed
with serious pizazz good! They'll
make the ideal accompaniment
to the punchy poultry you serve
during your Super Bowl blowout.
The crunchy texture contrasts
perfectly with the other recipes
in this chapter, and if there's
any chicken-wing sauce to mop
up, you'll know what to use.

Combine the vegetables, except the chilli, in a large bowl or pan.

In a heatproof bowl, cover the chilli/chile, if using, with boiling water and let stand for about 10 minutes. Drain and transfer to a large saucepan. Add the remaining ingredients and 700 ml/ 3 cups water and bring to a boil, stirring to dissolve the sugar.

Cover the top of the bowl containing the vegetables with a muslin/ cheesecloth, then pour the hot liquid over the contents. Ball up the sifted spices in the muslin/cheesecloth, tie at the top and submerge in the pickling mixture. Cover the vegetables and pickling liquid with a plate, let cool to room temperature, then cover with clingfilm/plastic wrap and refrigerate for 2–3 days.

Drain the vegetables and serve on a platter. Alternatively, transfer the vegetables to sterilized jars and top up with the pickling liquid. They'll keep in the fridge for up to 2 weeks.

# FRIED GAME HEN & CORNMEAL WAFFLES

4 small Cornish game hens (Rock hen
   or Poussin)
1 litre/quart buttermilk
1 large white onion, roughly chopped
2 tablespoons chopped garlic
1 bunch of thyme sprigs
1–2 tablespoons hot sauce
4 litres/4 quarts rapeseed/canola or ground
   nut/peanut oil
4 whole garlic cloves, peeled
1 teaspoon salt
135 g/1 cup plain/all-purpose flour
1 tablespoon cayenne pepper
45 g/³/₄ cup panko breadcrumbs
a pinch of paprika

**CORNMEAL WAFFLES**
135 g/1 cup plain/all-purpose flour
150 g/1 cup yellow polenta/cornmeal
2 teaspoons baking powder
¹/₂ teaspoon bicarbonate of soda/baking soda
¹/₄ teaspoon salt
300 ml/1¹/₄ cups buttermilk
2 eggs
115 g/1 stick unsalted butter, melted

*4-litre/quart casserole dish/Dutch oven*
*a deep-fat thermometer*
*kitchen string/twine*
*a waffle iron*
*non-stick cooking spray, for oiling*

**Serves 4**

Remove any visible fat from the birds, rinse under cold water
and pat dry. Combine the buttermilk, onion, chopped garlic, eight
of the thyme sprigs and the hot sauce in a large bowl.

Add the hens, turning to coat. Cover and marinate in the fridge for
6–12 hours.

Heat the oil in the casserole dish/Dutch oven fitted with a deep-fat
thermometer over medium-high heat to 180°C (350°F). Remove the
hens from the marinade and pat dry with paper towels. Place one
garlic clove and the remaining thyme sprigs in each hen's cavity, tie
the legs together with kitchen string/twine and sprinkle the hens
with the salt.

Mix the flour and cayenne together in a medium bowl. Dredge
the hens first in the seasoned flour and then in the panko, patting
off the excess flour. Fry one at a time for 10 minutes until crispy,
golden brown and cooked through. Drain on a wire rack and let rest
for 10 minutes while you prepare the waffles.

Preheat the oven to 110°C (225°F) Gas 4 to keep the waffles warm
after they are cooked.

In a medium mixing bowl, mix the dry ingredients together. In
another bowl, beat the all the wet ingredients together, including
the melted butter. Pour the wet into the dry and mix just until they
are combined.

Lightly spray your waffle iron with non-stick cooking spray
and pour in about 125 ml/¹/₂ cup batter for each waffle. Cook until
browned and crisp. Place in oven to keep warm while cooking the
other waffles. Serve the warm hens with the waffles as soon
as they are cooked.

# BEER MARGARITA

350-ml/12-fl. oz. can 'frozen' limeade
    concentrate or 350 ml/1½ cups
    Homemade Limeade Concentrate
    (see below)
350 ml/1½ cups tequila
350 ml/1½ cups beer
1 tablespoon sea salt
ice cubes
1 lime, cut into wedges, to garnish

HOMEMADE LIMEADE CONCENTRATE
300 g/1½ cups white sugar
350 ml/1½ cups freshly squeezed
    lime juice

**Makes 4**

If making the Limeade Concentrate, put the sugar into a saucepan with 350 ml/1½ cups water. Heat gently over low heat, stirring occasionally, until the sugar has dissolved. Add the lime juice and stir well. Let cool, then freeze.

To make the beer margarita, combine the limeade, tequila and beer in a large jug/pitcher with 350 ml/1½ cups water. Stir until the limeade has melted and everything has combined.

Place the sea salt on a plate. Dampen the rims of the glasses, then dip them in the salt. Add a handful of ice cubes to each glass, pour over the beer margarita and, if liked, garnish with a lime wedge to serve.

# HOMEMADE LEMON-LIME SODA

400 g/2 cups white sugar
2 lemons, sliced
2 limes, sliced
1 lime, cut into wedges,
    to garnish

ice cubes
soda water/club soda,
    to serve

**Makes 4–6**

In a medium-sized saucepan, combine the sugar, lemons and limes with 450 ml/2 cups water. Bring to a boil over medium heat and boil for 5 minutes. Remove from the heat and let cool, then strain.

Add a few ice cubes to each glass, dilute 1–2 tablespoons of the syrup with 225 ml/1 cup soda water/club soda and garnish with a lime wedge to serve.

# NO MESSING BOARD GAMES NIGHT

Get your game face on with these winning wonders. Your guests/ competition will be so distracted by your tasty treats as they munch over Monopoly, chew over Cluedo, pick over Pictionary and sip over Scrabble, that you can swoop in for the win during your 'friendly' game of whatever you're playing. One word of advice, though: don't even attempt to play Twister on a full stomach – that's surely a recipe for disaster.

## SMALL PLATES & SIDES
Olive Oil & Black Pepper Nibbles
Chorizo, Red Pepper & Pea Frittata Squares
Spiced Mixed Nuts
Crispy Pork Belly Bites

## BIGGER BITES
Artichoke, Olive & Provolone Panini

## SOMETHING SWEET
Chocolate Bites with Whisky & Blood Orange Cream

## DRINKS
Classic Dry Martini

# OLIVE OIL & BLACK PEPPER NIBBLES

150 g /1 cup plus 3 tablespoons Italian '00'
    flour, plus extra for dusting and kneading
40 g/¼ cup semolina (fine)
1 teaspoon freshly ground black pepper
2 teaspoons fine sea salt
70 ml/⅓ cup dry white wine
70 ml/⅓ cup extra virgin olive oil
olive oil, for oiling

**MAKES 30**

Put the flour, semolina, pepper and half the salt
in a large bowl. Add the wine and oil and mix to
combine. Turn out onto a floured surface and knead
for about 2 minutes until the dough is smooth and
elastic. Place the dough in a lightly oiled bowl, cover
with a clean tea/kitchen towel and let rest for
about 45 minutes to 1 hour.

Halve the dough and cut each half into 10 pieces.
Keep the remaining dough covered as you work
to stop it drying out. Roll one piece of dough into
a 50-cm/20-inch long rope. Cut the rope into five
pieces, then roll each piece into a 10-cm/4-inch rope.

Connect the ends to form an overlapping ring.
Continue with the remaining dough, keeping the
rings covered too, as you make them.

Preheat the oven to 180°C (350°F) Gas 4. In a large
saucepan, bring 900 ml/scant 4 cups water to a boil
and add the remaining salt.

Add the rings to the saucepan of boiling water
in batches and cook for about 3 minutes until they
float. Use a slotted spoon to transfer them to two
oiled baking sheets. Bake in the preheated oven for
about 30 minutes until golden and crisp. Let cool
on wire racks before serving with drinks.

# CHORIZO, RED PEPPER & PEA FRITTATA SQUARES

4 cooking chorizo sausages
    (about 60 g/2¼ oz.)
16 eggs
300 ml/1¼ cups crème fraîche/sour cream
1 tablespoon olive oil
150 g/1 cup (about 1 medium) finely chopped
    red onion
1 garlic clove, crushed
130 g/1 cup fresh or frozen peas
1 red (bell) pepper, seeded and cut
    into strips
60 g/2 cups baby spinach
a pinch of salt and freshly ground
    black pepper, to season

**SERVES 8–10**

Preheat the oven to 180°C (350°F) Gas 4.

Place the chorizo sausages on a baking sheet and cook in the preheated oven for 12 minutes. Remove from the oven, drain on paper towels and cut into 1-cm/½-inch slices. Cover and set aside.

Reduce the oven temperature to 110°C (225°F) Gas ¼. Put the eggs in a large mixing bowl with the crème fraîche/sour cream and lightly beat to combine. Season with salt and pepper and set aside.

Heat the olive oil in a large non-stick, ovenproof frying pan/skillet set over low-medium heat. Add the onion and garlic and sauté until soft but not coloured.

Add the sliced chorizo, peas and (bell) pepper strips and cook for 2–3 minutes, stirring occasionally.

Add the baby spinach and stir until the spinach just begins to wilt.

Arrange the mix evenly over the bottom of the pan and carefully pour in the egg mixture.

Reduce the heat and gently cook the frittata, moving the egg in a little from the edge of the pan as it cooks (similar to how you would cook an omelette), using a spatula to run around the outside of the pan. You don't want to get any colour on the bottom of the frittata, so it is key to keep the temperature low.

Continue running the spatula around the outside of the pan to ensure the frittata doesn't stick.

After about 10 minutes, once it has just set on the bottom and the sides, place the pan in the oven for 15–20 minutes until the frittata is lightly golden and just set in the middle. Remove from the oven and let cool for 10 minutes.

Once cool, cover the pan with a chopping/cutting board and turn it over to release the frittata. Cut it into 4-cm/1½-inch squares and transfer to a plate to serve.

# SPICED MIXED NUTS

500 g/3¾ cups assorted unsalted nuts
   (cashews, hazelnuts, Brazil nuts, peanuts,
   blanched almonds, pecans, walnuts)
1 tablespoon fennel seeds
2 tablespoons sesame seeds
100 g/¾ cup pumpkin seeds
1½ tablespoons (about 2 sprigs)
   coarsely chopped rosemary
1 teaspoon dried chilli/hot red pepper flakes
4 teaspoons dark muscovado/packed dark
   brown sugar
1 teaspoon sea salt
2 tablespoons melted unsalted butter

**MAKES 650 G (43 OZ.)/4¾ CUPS**

Preheat the oven to 180°C (350°F) Gas 4.

Spread the nuts on a baking sheet. Toast in the preheated oven for about 10 minutes until lightly golden brown.

Meanwhile, place the fennel, sesame and pumpkin seeds in a preheated frying pan/skillet set over medium heat. Dry-fry the seeds for a few minutes until the sesame seeds turn golden brown.

Put the rosemary, dried chilli/hot red pepper flakes, sugar, salt and melted butter in a large mixing bowl and stir to combine.

While the nuts and seeds are still warm from the oven and pan, toss in the butter spice mixture to coat thoroughly.

# ARTICHOKE, OLIVE & PROVOLONE PANINI

4 slices panini bread
unsalted butter, melted, for brushing
1–2 tablespoons sun-dried tomato paste
180 g/6 oz. Provolone cheese, grated/
   shredded or thinly sliced
6–8 marinated artichoke hearts, drained
   and sliced
65 g/½ cup pitted green olives,
   coarsely chopped
½ teaspoon dried oregano

*panini press*

**SERVES 2**

Preheat the panini press. Brush melted butter on the bread slices on one side. Spread two of the slices with the sun-dried tomato paste on the non-buttered side and set aside.

Top the other two slices of bread with half of the cheese. Arrange the artichoke hearts on top and sprinkle with the olives and oregano.

Sprinkle over the remaining cheese and cover with the other bread slices, tomato side down.

Toast in the preheated panini press for 2–3 minutes or according to the manufacturer's instructions. The bread should be golden brown and the filling completely warmed through.

Cut each panini into quarters before serving.

# CRISPY PORK BELLY BITES

85 g/¼ cup honey
5 bay leaves
3 rosemary sprigs
250 g/1 cup sea salt
2 tablespoons black peppercorns
1 small bunch of thyme
1 garlic bulb, cloves removed and flattened
   with skin on
1.5 kg/3 lbs. 5 oz. lbs. pork belly, skin on
2 litres/quarts olive oil
roughly chopped coriander/cilantro,
   to garnish

*a baking sheet, oiled and lined
   with parchment paper*

SERVES 8–10

Begin by brining the pork. Combine the honey, bay leaves, rosemary, salt, peppercorns, thyme, garlic and 3 litres/quarts water in a container large enough to hold the pork.

Place the pork in the brine, cover and set in the fridge for at least 12 hours or overnight.

Remove the pork from the brine and discard the brine. Rinse the pork in a large bowl under running water, then pat dry with paper towels.

To confit the pork, preheat the oven to 120°C (250°F) Gas ½. Place the rinsed pork in a roasting pan and pour over the olive oil. Cover with foil and cook in the preheated oven for 4½ hours. The oil will gently bubble and poach the pork until it is soft and falling apart.

Remove from the oven, uncover slightly and let the pork cool to room temperature.

Press the pork so that it has a nice, firm texture by removing it from the oil and placing it, rind side down, on the prepared baking sheet. Reserve the oil

for crisping the skin later. Cover the pork with clingfilm/plastic wrap and weigh it down with something heavy like a big wooden chopping/cutting board or a cast-iron roasting dish. Set in the fridge for at least 12 hours.

When ready to serve, preheat the oven to 220°C (425°F) Gas 7.

Score the skin of the pressed pork with a diamond pattern and cut into 2-cm/¾-inch squares.

Drizzle a clean baking sheet with a little of the reserved cooking oil, place the pork squares skin side down and roast for 15 minutes until the skin is golden brown and crisp.

Remove from the oven and drain on paper towels. Alternatively, you can crisp up the skin by placing the pork, skin side up, underneath a grill/broiler on medium heat for 3–4 minutes.

Transfer to a serving platter and garnish with chopped coriander/cilantro.

# CHOCOLATE BITES WITH WHISKY & BLOOD ORANGE CREAM

250 g/2¼ sticks unsalted butter, chopped
200 g/7 oz. dark/bittersweet chocolate,
    chopped
250 ml/1 cup full-fat/whole milk
80 ml/⅓ cup whisky or brandy
330 g/1⅔ cups caster/granulated sugar
1 teaspoon pure vanilla extract
1 teaspoon instant coffee
3 eggs
200 g/1⅔ cups plain/all-purpose flour
60 g/2 oz. self-raising/rising flour
25 g/3½ tablespoons cocoa powder,
    plus extra for dusting
candied oranges, to serve (optional)

CHOCOLATE GANACHE ICING/FROSTING
150 g/5½ oz. dark/bittersweet chocolate,
    chopped
1–2 teaspoons golden/light corn syrup,
125 ml/½ cup double/heavy cream

WHISKY & BLOOD ORANGE CREAM
200 ml/¾ cup double/heavy cream
20 ml/4 teaspoons whisky or brandy
juice of 1 blood orange
2–3 tablespoons caster/superfine sugar

28 x 20-cm/11 x 8-inch baking pan,
    lightly greased

SERVES 10

Preheat the oven to 150°C (300°F) Gas 2.

Place the butter, chocolate, milk, whisky or brandy, sugar, vanilla and coffee in a large saucepan over medium heat and stir occasionally for 6 minutes or until melted and smooth. Set aside to cool slightly. Add the eggs and beat to combine. Pour into a large bowl, sift in the flours and cocoa and beat until smooth.

Pour into the prepared baking pan and bake in the preheated oven for 40 minutes or until cooked when tested with a skewer. Let cool completely in the baking pan, then remove.

To make the chocolate ganache icing/frosting, heat the chocolate, syrup and cream in a small saucepan over low heat, stirring, until melted and smooth. Set aside to cool completely.

Meanwhile, for the blood orange cream, whip the cream, whisky or brandy, blood orange juice and sugar until light and fluffy and set aside.

When the cake has cooled, spread the chocolate ganache icing/frosting over the top and let set. Cut into bite-sized squares and either top with the blood orange cream or serve it on the side, along with the candied oranges, if you like.

# CLASSIC DRY MARTINI

60 ml/2 fl. oz. gin
a dash of dry vermouth
ice cubes
green olive, to garnish

MAKES 1

Using a mixing glass, chill the gin and vermouth over ice, and pour into a frosted martini glass. Garnish with a green olive.

# VALENTINE'S DINNER DATE

Is your lover quite the dish? The way to a person's heart is most certainly through their stomach, so turn the lights down low, fire up some candles, play some soft music, and arouse curiosity with the cuisine you serve, ramping up the romance with each helping. On your Big Romantic Night In, love will most certainly be in the air, as will the appetising, aphrodisiac aromas of your deeply desirable food. Wanna spoon?

## SMALL PLATES & SIDES
Asparagus & Prosciutto Gratin

## BIGGER BITES
Risotto Nero with Prawns

## SOMETHING SWEET
Strawberry Shortcake Layer Mousses
Frangelico Truffles

## DRINKS
Babycakes

# ASPARAGUS & PROSCIUTTO GRATIN

12 asparagus spears
20 g/generous 1 tablespoon butter, plus
    extra for greasing
150 ml/²/₃ cup crème fraîche/sour cream
1 teaspoon chopped parsley
6 slices prosciutto
2 teaspoons breadcrumbs
2 teaspoons finely grated Parmesan cheese
sea salt and freshly ground black pepper,
    to season

**SERVES 2**

Bend each asparagus spear until it snaps, and discard the woody ends. Steam the asparagus spears over a pan of boiling water for about 3–4 minutes, just to soften them – you don't want them fully cooked. Set aside.

Meanwhile, melt the butter in a frying pan/skillet and then stir in the crème fraîche/sour cream. Add the chopped parsley, season with salt and pepper and remove from the heat.

Preheat the grill/broiler to medium. Wrap a slice of prosciutto around two asparagus spears and lay them in a greased ovenproof roasting dish. Repeat with the remaining prosciutto slices and asparagus spears, laying them side by side in the dish.

Pour the melted butter and crème fraîche/sour cream mixture evenly over the top. Mix the breadcrumbs and Parmesan cheese together in a bowl and then sprinkle this over the top.

Grill/broil for 6–8 minutes until nicely browned and slightly crisp on top. Serve immediately.

# RISOTTO NERO WITH PRAWNS

1 litre/quart good-quality fish stock
3 tablespoons olive oil
1 shallot, finely chopped
3 garlic cloves, 2 finely chopped and
    1 peeled but left whole
200-g/7-oz. squid, cleaned and chopped
    into small pieces
8-g/¼-fl .oz. sachet of squid ink
350 g/1¾ cups risotto rice
50 ml/3½ tablespoons dry white wine
25 g/2 tablespoons butter
12 raw tiger prawns/shrimp,
    heads removed, peeled and deveined
salt, to season
chopped parsley, to garnish

**SERVES 4**

Bring the fish stock to a simmer in a large pan.

Heat 2 tablespoons of the olive oil in a separate saucepan. Add the shallot and finely chopped garlic and fry gently, stirring, until the shallot has softened. Add the squid and fry until whitened and opaque. Mix in the squid ink and the rice. Pour in the wine and cook, stirring, until reduced. Add a ladleful of the stock to the rice and cook, stirring, until absorbed. Repeat the process until all the stock has been added and the rice is cooked through. Season with salt as needed. Stir in the butter and set aside to rest.

Heat the remaining oil in a frying pan/skillet. Add the whole garlic clove and fry, stirring, until fragrant. Add the prawns/shrimp with a pinch of salt and fry, stirring, until they have turned pink and opaque and cooked through. Discard the garlic clove.

Serve each portion of the risotto rice topped with the prawns/shrimp and garnished with chopped parsley.

# STRAWBERRY SHORTCAKE LAYER MOUSSES

**MOUSSE**
3 sheets of leaf gelatine (platinum grade
    available in supermarkets)
400 g/14 oz. ripe strawberries, hulled
    and sliced
100 g/½ cup caster/granulated sugar
½ teaspoon vanilla bean powder or vanilla
    bean paste
grated zest and juice of 1 lemon
300 ml/1¼ cups double/heavy cream
80 g/⅓ cup cream cheese

**CHEESECAKE CRUMB LAYER**
200 g/7 oz. shortcake biscuits/cookies
100 g/7 tablespoons butter

**TO ASSEMBLE**
300 g/10½ oz. ripe strawberries
150 ml/⅔ cup double/heavy cream

2 piping/pastry bags, fitted with large
    round nozzles/tips
6 pretty glasses

**SERVES 6**

Soak the gelatine leaves in cold water until soft. This will take about 5 minutes.

Place the strawberries, sugar, vanilla and lemon zest and juice a in a saucepan with 100 ml/⅓ cup water and heat for about 5 minutes until the strawberries are very soft. Pass the mixture through a sieve/strainer, pressing down on the strawberries firmly with the back of a spoon so that they become a fruit purée. Discard any strawberries remaining in the sieve/strainer. Squeeze the water out of the gelatine leaves and add to the warm strawberry syrup.

Stir until dissolved, then pass through the sieve/strainer again to remove any undissolved gelatine pieces. Let cool. Whip the double/heavy cream and cream cheese together and then whisk in the strawberry syrup.

In a food processor or blender, blitz the shortcake biscuits/cookies to fine crumbs. Melt the butter and then stir into the crumbs to ensure they are all coated.

To assemble, reserve three strawberries for decoration, then hull and slice the rest. Place a large spoonful of crumbs into the bottom of each glass and then top each with several slices of the strawberries. Spoon the strawberry mousse into one piping/pastry bag and pipe a generous swirl of mousse into the glasses. Repeat with a second layer of crumbs, strawberries and mousse and then let chill in the fridge for 3 hours or ideally overnight.

To serve, whip the 150 ml/⅔ cup double/heavy cream to stiff peaks, then spoon into the second piping/pastry bag and pipe small swirls of cream around the edge of each mousse. Decorate each glass with a reserved strawberry half to finish.

# FRANGELICO TRUFFLES

200 g/7 oz. dark/
    bittersweet (70%)
    chocolate, chopped
200 ml/³/₄ cup double/
    heavy cream
5 tablespoons Frangelico
a pinch of salt

1 teaspoon vanilla bean paste
15 g/1 tablespoon unsalted
    butter
cocoa powder, for dusting

15 x 12.5-cm/6 x 5-inch
    plastic container

**MAKES 25**

Put the chocolate in a heatproof bowl. Bring the cream to a gentle simmer and then pour over the chocolate. Let stand for 30 seconds.

Whip the cream and chocolate together, then add the rest of the ingredients except the cocoa powder and stir together.

Line the plastic container with clingfilm/plastic wrap and pour in the chocolate mix. Refrigerate overnight.

Turn out the truffle onto a board and use a sharp knife to cut it into squares. Dust with cocoa powder.

These truffles can be stored in an airtight container in the fridge for up to 1 week. Dust with extra cocoa powder before serving. They also freeze well.

# BABYCAKES

15 ml/¹/₂ fl. oz. vodka
10 ml/¹/₃ fl. oz. Chambord
10 ml/¹/₃ fl. oz. crème de
    fraise des bois or other
    strawberry liqueur
¹/₂ teaspoon rosewater
ice cubes
well-chilled Asti Spumante
    or other semi-sweet
    sparkling wine, to
    top up

edible rose petal or
    strawberry, halved,
    to garnish (optional)
Iced Gems or other
    sweets/candies, to serve
    (optional)

**MAKES 1**

Pour the first four ingredients into an ice-filled cocktail shaker and stir well. Strain into a chilled Champagne flute and top up with Asti Spumante. Garnish with a rose petal or halved strawberry, if you like, and serve with Iced Gems or other sweets/candies.

# COSY COMFORT FOOD

Enjoying good food with good friends is like a huge welcoming blanket being wrapped around you. It's probably like swimming in hot chocolate or snuggling into a fluffy towel fresh from the tumble dryer. Hearty soup, a steaming hotpot, a fruity tart... this chapter has 'em all, and then some. So laugh, reminisce and regale tales with your pals as you tuck into these heart-warming – and belly-warming – hugs on a plate. There is no doubt, contentment is guaranteed.

## SMALL PLATES & SIDES

Leek & Potato Soup

Herb Spelt Bread

Garlic & Almond Sprouting Broccoli

## BIGGER BITES

Lancashire Hotpot

## SOMETHING SWEET

Rhubarb Tart

## DRINKS

Hot Toddy

# LEEK & POTATO SOUP

700 g/1 lb. 9 oz. leeks
50 g/3½ tablespoons butter
200 g/7 oz. potatoes, peeled and cubed
50 ml/3½ tablespoons dry white wine
800 ml/3⅓ cups good chicken stock,
    ideally homemade
200 ml/¾ cup double/heavy cream, plus
    extra to garnish
freshly grated nutmeg, to season
salt and freshly ground black pepper,
    to season
chopped chives, to garnish
croûtons, to serve (optional)

**SERVES 4**

Trim the leeks, discarding their tough outer casing and dark green tops. Finely chop and rinse thoroughly to get rid of any soil trapped between the layers.

Melt the butter in a large, heavy-bottomed saucepan over low heat. Add in the leeks and fry very gently for 10 minutes, stirring often so as to prevent them from scorching.

Add in the cubed potatoes, mixing well. Pour in the wine, increase the heat to medium and cook for a few minutes, stirring now and then, until most of the wine has evaporated. Add in the chicken stock and season with salt and pepper. Bring to a boil, then reduce the heat and simmer for 25 minutes until the potatoes are tender.

Blend the soup thoroughly until smooth, then stir in the cream and season with freshly grated nutmeg. Serve each portion garnished with a swirl of cream, a sprinkling of chives, freshly ground black pepper and croûtons, if you like.

# HERB SPELT BREAD

500 g/4⅓ cups wholegrain spelt flour, plus
    extra for sprinkling and kneading
2 teaspoons sea salt
3 teaspoons coarsely chopped rosemary
2 teaspoons freshly ground black pepper
2 tablespoons rapeseed/canola oil
1 tablespoon fragrant honey, such as acacia
    or rosemary honey
7 g/¼ oz. fresh yeast or 1 teaspoon dried
    active/active dry yeast
400 ml/1¾ cups water at body temperature
    (you will need to adjust the quantity
    if using white spelt)

*a baking sheet lined with parchment paper*

**MAKES 2 BAGUETTES**

In a large bowl, add the flour, salt, rosemary and black pepper and mix well. Make a well in the middle of the flour mixture and add the oil and honey and then the yeast and water.

Mix well and turn out of the bowl onto a lightly floured work surface. Knead, adding more flour as necessary. The dough should be strong, soft and silky. Knead for approximately 8 minutes.

Shape into two baguettes and place on the prepared baking sheet side by side. Cover and let rest for 40 minutes.

Preheat the oven to 180°C (350°F) Gas 4. Bake the loaves until they are golden brown and sound hollow when you tap the underside. Cool on a wire rack.

Enjoy with butter or the Leek & Potato Soup (see above), or dipped in oil.

# LANCASHIRE HOTPOT

2 tablespoons lard or
    goose fat or vegetable
    or sunflower oil
8 thick-cut lamb chops
2 turnips, peeled and
    chopped into chunks
2 carrots, peeled, halved
    lengthways and cut into
    2.5-cm/1-inch pieces
2 leeks, washed and
    thinly sliced
1 tablespoon chopped
    parsley, plus extra
    to garnish

450 g/1 lb. potatoes,
    peeled and very thinly
    sliced
600 ml/2½ cups lamb,
    beef or chicken stock
25 g/2 tablespoons butter,
    melted
salt and freshly ground
    black pepper, to season

**Serves 4**

Preheat the oven to 200°C (400°F) Gas 6.

Heat the lard, goose fat or oil in a large frying pan/
skillet. Fry the lamb chops until lightly browned on
both sides and then season with salt and black
pepper. Remove from the heat.

Layer the ingredients in a heavy-bottomed casserole
dish, seasoning the layers with salt and pepper
as you do so, as follows. First, place half the turnips,
carrots and leeks in the bottom of the dish. Top with
the lamp chops, sprinkling them with the parsley.
Layer with the remaining turnips, carrots and leeks.
Layer the potato slices over the vegetables,
overlapping the slices.

Pour the stock into the casserole and, on the hob/
stovetop, bring to a boil.

Brush the potato topping with the melted butter.
Cover the casserole and bake in the preheated oven
for 1¾ hours. Uncover the casserole and bake for an
additional 15 minutes until the potatoes are golden.
Garnish with parsley and serve.

# GARLIC & ALMOND
# SPROUTING BROCCOLI

300 g/10½ oz. purple
    sprouting broccoli,
    chopped into 2.5-cm/
    1-inch lengths, or
    broccoli florets
25 g/¼ cup flaked/slivered
    almonds

2 tablespoons olive oil
1 large garlic clove, roughly
    chopped
salt and freshly ground
    black pepper, to season

**Serves 4**

Bring a large pan of salted water to a boil. Add the
broccoli and cook for 2 minutes, then drain and
refresh in cold water to stop the cooking process.

Dry-fry the almonds in a frying pan/skillet, stirring
often, until golden brown; set aside.

Heat the oil in a large frying pan/skillet. Add the
garlic and fry until golden. Add the drained broccoli
and fry for 2 minutes, stirring to coat in the oil. Add
the almonds, season with pepper and serve at once.

# RHUBARB TART

150 g/1 cup plus 3 tablespoons plain/all-purpose flour
1 teaspoon baking powder
100 g/7 tablespoons unsalted butter, softened at room temperature and diced
85 g/scant ½ cup caster/superfine sugar
1 egg yolk

**FILLING**
300 g/10½ oz. rhubarb, trimmed and roughly chopped

2 tablespoons soft/packed dark brown sugar
50 g/3½ tablespoons unsalted butter, softened at room temperature and diced
60 g/⅓ cup caster sugar
50 g/scant ½ cup old-fashioned rolled (porridge) oats

a 20-cm/8-inch fluted tart pan with a removable bottom, greased

**SERVES 6–8**

Preheat the oven to 200°C (400°F) Gas 6.

Sift the flour and baking powder into a mixing bowl. Rub the butter into the flour mixture with your fingertips until it looks like breadcrumbs. Stir in the sugar and egg yolk and mix until a dough forms.

Transfer the dough to the tart pan and push and press it into the pan until the bottom and sides are evenly covered with a neat layer of dough.

To make the filling, put the rhubarb and brown sugar in a bowl and mix until the rhubarb is evenly coated, then transfer to the pastry case/shell and spread roughly over the bottom of the tart.

In a separate bowl, mix the butter, caster/superfine sugar and oats together until you have a mixture like a crumble topping. Scatter roughly over the rhubarb filling.

Bake in the preheated oven for 30 minutes or until the crumble topping and pastry are golden brown.

# HOT TODDY

5 whole cloves
2 lemon slices
60 ml/2 fl. oz. whisky
30 ml/1 fl. oz. freshly squeezed lemon juice

2 teaspoons honey or simple syrup
90 ml/3 fl. oz. hot water
1 cinnamon stick

**MAKES 1**

Spear the cloves into the lemon slices and add them to a heatproof glass or a toddy glass along with the rest of the ingredients.

# INDOOR PICNIC

Al fresco picnicking is all very well and good but, let's be honest, it's
a bit of a hassle to load everything into a hamper, lug it to 'the perfect spot',
then battle the bugs as you try to enjoy your Scotch egg. And that's before
the heavens open and you're left with soggy sandwiches. Take this palaver
out of the equation and lay a rug in your living room (or a chequered
tablecloth on a table to keep this a classier, not-sitting-on-the-floor affair).
Warning: don't try to play frisbee.

## SMALL PLATES & SIDES
Scotch Quails' Eggs
Grilled Halloumi with Jalapeño Relish
Herbed Crushed Potatoes
Rosemary Skewered Sausages

## BIGGER BITES
Spring Pasta Salad Jar
Salad of Roasted Vegetables

## SOMETHING SWEET
Lemon Drizzle Cake

## DRINKS
Pimm's Deluxe

# SCOTCH QUAILS' EGGS

12 quails' eggs
600 g/1¼ lbs. good-quality pork sausages
1 tablespoon finely chopped parsley
1 tablespoon finely chopped thyme (optional)
1 egg yolk, beaten, plus 1 whole egg
1 tablespoon plain/all-purpose flour

4 tablespoons/1¼ cups milk
75 g/1¼ cups fine breadcrumbs
sunflower oil, for deep-frying
sea salt and ground black pepper, to season

**MAKES 12**

Bring a saucepan of water to a boil and gently lower in the quails' eggs. Boil for 100 seconds, then plunge the boiled eggs immediately into cold water to stop additional cooking. Once cold, one at a time, roll each egg gently along a work surface with the flat of your palm until the shell is all crackled, then peel away the shell. Set the peeled eggs aside until needed.

Remove the skins from the sausages and discard and put the sausage meat in a large mixing bowl with the parsley, thyme, if using, and egg yolk. Season with salt and pepper and stir to combine. Divide the mixture into 12 equal portions.

Now get three shallow bowls ready, the first holding the plain/all-purpose flour seasoned with salt and pepper, the next with a whole egg beaten with the milk and the last bowl filled with the breadcrumbs.

Take a portion of sausage meat and make a patty with it in your palm. Place a quail's egg in the centre and gently mould the sausage meat around it before rolling it into a ball between your palms. Repeat with the rest of the sausage meat and quails' eggs. Roll each Scotch egg firstly in seasoned flour, then dip it in the egg wash before coating it in the breadcrumbs.

Pour the oil for deep-frying into a large pan and bring up to smoking hot temperature (around 180°C/350°F) or until a small piece of bread brown in 60 seconds. Fry a few eggs at a time for about 4 minutes until they are golden brown all over. Transfer to a plate lined with paper towels to soak up any excess oil and let cool before serving.

# GRILLED HALLOUMI WITH JALAPEÑO RELISH

450 g/1 lb. halloumi
3 tablespoons olive oil
grated zest and juice
  of 2 limes
Jalapeño Relish (see
  below)
cracked black pepper,
  for sprinkling
extra limes, for squeezing

**JALAPEÑO RELISH**
  (makes 475 ml/2 cups)
4 jalapeño chillies/chiles
3 tablespoons olive oil,
  plus extra for oiling

1 red and 1 white onion,
  thinly sliced
3 garlic cloves, finely
  chopped
1 tablespoon lime pickle
2 tablespoons tequila
3 tablespoons honey
60 ml/¼ cup white wine
  vinegar
sea salt flakes, to season

*still-warm sterilized glass
  jars with airtight lids*

**SERVES 6**

Begin with the halloumi. Slice the cheese into
5-mm/¼-inch pieces. Place a cast-iron pan over
medium heat and add the olive oil. Add the halloumi
and sauté on each side for 2 minutes.

Add a little lime zest and juice to the pan for each
batch. The halloumi will cook quickly, so don't let
it brown too much. Transfer the cheese to a warm
serving platter until needed.

To make the relish, place a lightly oiled large cast-iron
pan over high heat until smoking. Add the jalapeños,
lower the heat slightly and cook until the skins are
charred and blistered. Remove from the pan and set
aside to cool.

Add the oil, sliced onions and garlic to the pan and cook
over medium heat for 5 minutes, stirring occasionally.
Season with salt to taste. Add the lime pickle.

Roughly chop the jalapeños and add to the pan with
the tequila, honey and vinegar. Cook for an additional
10 minutes until the onions are golden and soft.

To serve, place a teaspoon of relish on top of each
piece of cheese. Sprinkle with black pepper and
an extra squeeze of lime.

# HERBED CRUSHED POTATOES

500 g/1 lb. 2 oz. even-sized
  waxy potatoes
2 tablespoons extra virgin
  olive oil
grated zest of ½ lemon
1 teaspoon freshly
  squeezed lemon juice
2 tablespoons chopped
  chives

2 tablespoons chopped
  mint leaves
3 tablespoons finely
  chopped parsley
salt and freshly ground
  black pepper, to season

**SERVES 4**

Cook the potatoes in salted boiling water until
tender; drain.

Return the potatoes to the pan. Use a masher to
roughly crush them. Add the olive oil and lemon zest
and juice and season with the salt and pepper,
mixing well. Add the chives, mint and parsley and
mix in. Serve warm or at room temperature.

# SPRING PASTA SALAD JAR

100 g/scant 1 cup fusilli
  pasta
4 tablespoons/¼ cup
  extra virgin olive oil
75 g/½ cup fresh or
  frozen peas
a small handful of
  mangetout/snowpeas,
  trimmed
½ courgette/zucchini,
  trimmed
a small handful of
  rocket/arugula

50 g/⅓ cup pistachios
2 tablespoons chopped
  mint leaves
½ small garlic clove,
  crushed
juice of ½ lemon
salt and freshly ground
  black pepper, to season

*a sterilized 1-litre/quart
  Kilner/Mason jar*

**Makes 1 jar**

Cook the pasta according to the instructions on the package until al dente. Drain well and immediately refresh under cold water. Drain again and dry well. Combine with a little of the olive oil.

Blanch the peas in lightly salted boiling water for 1 minute. Drain and refresh under cold water and drain again. Shake dry.

Thinly shred the mangetout/snowpeas and use a spiralizer (or grater) to spiralize or shred the courgette/zucchini.

Place the rocket/arugula, pistachios, mint, garlic, salt and pepper and half the remaining olive oil in a food processor and blend until smooth. Combine the remaining oil with the lemon juice and season to taste.

Next, arrange the pasta, vegetables and half the pesto in layers in the Kilner/Mason jar. Pour in the lemon dressing, cover the top with a circle of parchment paper and seal the jar. Chill in the fridge until required.

Note: This recipe makes twice the quantity of pesto needed, so use half and store the rest in an airtight container in the fridge for up to 3 days.

# SALAD OF ROASTED VEGETABLES

2 beet(root)s, peeled and sliced
2 parsnips, peeled and cut into batons
1 red onion, skin on, cut into wedges
½ small celeriac/celery root, peeled and cut into small chunks
2 tablespoons olive oil
2–3 teaspoons honey
1 tablespoon thyme leaves
1 cooking chorizo sausage (about 55 g/2 oz.), cubed (optional)
a big of handful rocket/arugula leaves
75 g/2½ oz. goats' cheese, crumbled
1–2 teaspoons balsamic vinegar
a handful of parsley, roughly chopped
sea salt and ground black pepper, to season

**SERVES 2–4**

Preheat the oven to 200°C (400°F) Gas 6.

Put the vegetables in a baking pan, drizzle with the olive oil and honey, season and sprinkle over the thyme leaves. Toss to coat the vegetables, put the pan in the oven and roast for 30–35 minutes until the vegetables are golden and caramelized. Remove from the oven, toss again in the hot oil in the pan, then let cool.

In a small frying pan/skillet, dry-fry the cubes of chorizo sausage until lightly browned around the edges. Let cool.

Transfer the cooled vegetables to a large mixing bowl, making sure you discard the outer layer or two of red onion skin as you go. Add the chorizo and a little of the leftover chorizo oil. Toss in the rocket/arugula leaves, goats' cheese and balsamic vinegar. Season and then garnish with a generous sprinkling of the parsley.

# ROSEMARY SKEWERED SAUSAGES

12 pork sausages of your choice
12 long sprigs of fresh rosemary
1 tablespoon olive oil
chunks of baguette, to serve

French mustard, to serve (optional)

*a barbecue/grill*
*a metal or wooden skewer*

**SERVES 6**

Take a sausage and spear it lengthways with the skewer. Remove the skewer and slowly thread a rosemary branch through where the hole has been made. If the rosemary breaks do not worry, just thread the rest of the sprig into the sausage from the other side.

Repeat this process with the rest of the sausages and rosemary sprigs, then brush them with olive oil. Place the sausages on a hot barbecue/grill and cook for 10–15 minutes, turning occasionally to brown on all sides.

Serve the sausages in a torn baguette with some good French mustard, if liked, or simply hot off the barbecue.

# LEMON DRIZZLE CAKE

**CAKE**
110 g/1 stick unsalted
    butter, softened
175 g/³/4 cup plus
    2 tablespoons
    caster/granulated sugar
175 g/1¹/3 cups self-raising/
    rising flour, sifted
1 teaspoon baking powder
a pinch of salt
2 UK large/US extra-large
    eggs
4 tablespoons/¹/2 cup full-
    fat/whole milk
finely grated zest
    of 2 lemons

**TOPPING**
100 g/¹/2 cup caster/
    granulated sugar
juice of 2 lemons

a 900-g/2-lb. loaf pan
    lined with parchment
    paper

**SERVES 8–10**

Preheat the oven to 180°C (350°F) Gas 4.

Put all the cake ingredients except the lemon zest into a large mixing bowl and, using an electric hand mixer, thoroughly combine until the mixture is creamy and has a dropping consistency. Fold through the lemon zest and pour the cake batter into the prepared loaf pan. Level the top with a palette knife and bake for 30–35 minutes or until an inserted skewer comes out clean.

In the meantime, stir the sugar and lemon juice together in a jug/pitcher to make the drizzle topping. Once the cake has baked, remove it from the oven and stab it all over with a skewer to create lots of fine holes for the syrup to soak through. Pour the lemon syrup over the hot cake and let the cake cool completely in its pan on top of a wire rack before turning out.

# PIMM'S DELUXE

ice cubes
50 ml/1³/4 fl. oz. Pimm's
    No 1 Cup
dash of elderflower cordial
sliced strawberries,
    orange, lemon and
    cucumber

well-chilled Prosecco
    or other dry sparkling
    wine, to top up
a mint sprig

**MAKES 1**

Fill a collins glass with ice cubes and add the Pimm's, elderflower cordial and sliced fruit. Stir well, then half-fill with Prosecco. Stir gently, then top up with Prosecco. Lightly crush the mint sprig and drop it in the top. Serve.

Note: If serving lots of people, make a jug/pitcher of this ahead of time, which helps extract more flavour from the fruit, adding the ice, Prosecco and mint just before serving. For a 2-litre/quart jug/pitcher, use 750 ml/25 fl. oz. Prosecco, 400 ml/14 fl. oz. Pimm's and 50 ml/1³/4 fl. oz. elderflower cordial.

# INDEX

**A**

apples: apple, sage & Calvados chutney 84
apple slaw 108
dill & apple herring 68
aquavit, dill 72
artichoke, olive & Provolone panini 144
asparagus & prosciutto gratin 150
aubergine: baba ghanoush 63
avocados: avocado dips 14, 92, 100
avocado margarita 96
choco-avo mousse 96
everything avocado toast 95
peach & avocado panzanella 95

**B**

B-52 128
baba ghanoush 63
babycakes 154
bacon: tomato bacon gratin 80
beans: Bourbon baked beans 134
chorizo & bean burger 111
Mexican-style beans 14
beef: chorizo & bean burger 111
beer margarita 138
black cloud ear fungus: egg noodle, black cloud ear fungus & tofu salad 45
blueberry tart 72
Bourbon baked beans 134
bread: artichoke, olive & Provolone panini 144
bruschetta 34, 65
everything avocado toast 95
flatbreads 127
focaccia crostini 37
herb spelt bread 158
peach & avocado panzanella 95
broccoli, garlic & almond sprouting 161
bruschetta 34, 76
burgers, chorizo & bean 111
burritos, orange-braised pork 18

**C**

cabbage: chorizo & red cabbage salad 76
cake, lemon drizzle 172
cauliflower: buffalo cauliflower & chickpea bowl 103
celeriac remoulade 108
cheese: artichoke, olive & Provolone panini 144
blue cheese & walnut bites 85
grilled halloumi with jalapeño relish 167
halloumi & mushroom kebabs 124
little spinach & feta pastries 60
Manchego & olive pinchos 52
shredded pastry with cheese in lemon syrup 64
sun-blush tomato, orange & burrata salad 87
trio of honey-baked Camembert 87
cheesecake 88
chicken: chicken noodle soup 46
chicken tinga tacos 17
ham & chicken croquettes 53
not your Dad's BBQ wings 108
spicy grilled orange-honey mustard wings 132
Thai peanut wings 132
chickpeas: buffalo cauliflower & chickpea bowl 103
chickpea masala 28
falafel 63
chillies: chilli & lime garlic mayo 116
chilli popcorn 120
gosht aloo saag masala 29
Szechuan chilli dressing 42
chipotle dip, creamy 100
chocolate: choco-avo mousse 96

chocolate bites 146
churros 57
Frangelico truffles 154
chorizo: chorizo & bean burger 111
chorizo & red cabbage salad 76
chorizo in red wine 54
chorizo, red pepper & pea frittata squares 143
churros 57
chutney 84
coconut rice 25
cola 112
corn on the cob: elotes 17
cosmo, rose & pomegranate 64
crisps, root vegetable 92
croquettes, ham & chicken 53
crostini, focaccia 37
cucumber: tomato, cucumber & mint raita 30
tzatziki 63

**D**

dips 63, 92, 100, 124
dough balls, wild garlic 116
dressing, Szechuan chilli 42
duck: cured duck & mustard bruschetta 76
dumplings, steamed rice noodle 42

**E**

eggs: chorizo, red pepper & pea frittata squares 143
Hong Kong egg tart 48
Scotch eggs 80, 166
Spanish potato tortilla 54
elotes 17

**F**

falafel with tzatziki 63
figs: fig & honey ricotta cheesecake 88
fig chutney 84
fish see herring; salmon, etc
focaccia crostini 37
Frangelico truffles 154
fries 111, 116, 128
frittata squares, chorizo, red pepper & pea 143

fruit, aquafaba pavlova with 104

**G**

game hen & cornmeal waffles 137
gosht aloo saag masala 29
gratins: asparagus & prosciutto 150
tomato bacon 80
gravad lax 68
Greek rice-stuffed tomatoes 60
guacamole 14

**H**

ham & chicken croquettes 53
herring: dill & apple herring 68
mustard herring 68
Hong Kong egg tart 48
hot toddy 162
hotpot, Lancashire 161

**J**

jalapeño relish 167
Jerusalem artichokes 102
julep, peach 104

**K**

kebabs: cured pork 79
halloumi & mushroom 124
mini kebabs 127
koftes, lamb 124

**L**

lamb: gosht aloo saag masala 29
lamb koftes 124
Lancashire hotpot 161
mini kebabs 127
Lancashire hotpot 161
leek & potato soup 158
lemons: lemon drizzle cake 172
lemon-lime soda 138
Naani Maa's lemon pickle 30
lettuce cups, mushroom-filled 45

**M**

margaritas 20, 96, 138

martini, classic dry 146
masala: chickpea masala 28
  gosht aloo saag masala 29
mayo, chilli & lime garlic 116
meringues: aquafaba
  pavlova 104
Mexican-style beans 14
mousses: choco-avo 96
  strawberry shortcake layer
  153
mushrooms: halloumi &
  mushroom kebabs 124
  mushroom & Parma ham
  pizza 34
  mushroom-filled lettuce
  cups 45

N
Naani Maa's lemon pickle 30
Negroni 38
noodles: chicken noodle
  soup 46
  egg noodle, black cloud ear
  fungus & tofu salad 45
not your Dad's BBQ wings
  108
nuts, spiced mixed 144

O
olive oil: olive oil & black
  pepper nibbles 142
olives: artichoke, olive &
  Provolone panini 144
  Manchego & olive pinchos
  52

P
pakoras, potato 27
panini, artichoke, olive &
  Provolone 144
panzanella, peach &
  avocado 95
Parma ham: mushroom &
  Parma ham pizza 34
pasta: spring pasta salad
  jar 168
pastries: little spinach & feta
  pastries 60
  shredded pastry with
  cheese in lemon syrup 64
patatas bravas 52
pavlova, aquafaba 104
peaches: peach & avocado

panzanella 95
peach julep 104
peanut butter: Thai peanut
  wings 132
peppers: chorizo, red pepper
  & pea frittata squares 143
pickles 30, 135
Pimm's deluxe 172
pinchos, Manchego & olive
  52
pizzas 34–6
popcorn 120
pork: crispy pork belly bites
  145
  cured pork kebab skewers
  79
  orange-braised pork
  burritos 18
potatoes: creamy potato
  salad 71
  fries 116, 128
  gosht aloo saag masala 29
  herbed crushed potatoes
  167
  Lancashire hotpot 161
  leek & potato soup 158
  patatas bravas 52
  potato pakoras 27
  samosas 24
  Spanish potato tortilla 54
prawns: flowering Chinese
  prawns 46
  risotto nero with prawns
  150
prosciutto: asparagus &
  prosciutto gratin 150
  'Scotch eggs' 80

Q
quails' eggs: Scotch eggs
  80, 166

R
raita, tomato, cucumber &
  mint 30
relish, jalapeño 167
remoulade, celeriac 108
rhubarb tart 162
rice: black rice & salmon
  salad 71
  coconut rice 25
  Greek rice-stuffed
  tomatoes 60

risotto nero with prawns
  150
ricotta: fig & honey ricotta
  cheesecake 88
risotto nero with prawns 150
root beer float 112
rose & pomegranate cosmo
  64

S
salads: apple slaw 108
  black rice & salmon 71
  chorizo & red cabbage 76
  creamy potato 71
  egg noodle, black cloud ear
  fungus & tofu 45
  peach & avocado
  panzanella 95
  salad of roasted vegetables
  171
  spring pasta salad jar 168
  sun-blush tomato, orange
  & burrata 87
salmon: black rice & salmon
  salad 71
  gravad lax 68
salsa, roasted tomato 14
salumi chips 79
samosas 24
sangria straight up 53
Sardinian pizza 36
sausages: rosemary
  skewered sausages 171
  Scotch quails' eggs 166
scallops, steamed rice
  noodle dumplings with 42
Scotch eggs 80, 166
shortcake: strawberry
  shortcake layer mousses
  153
shrimp see prawns
slaw, apple 108
soda, lemon-lime 138
soups: chicken noodle 46
  leek & potato 158
Spanish potato tortilla 54
spinach: little spinach & feta
  pastries 60
spring pasta salad jar 168
spritz, the perfect 38
strawberry shortcake layer
  mousses 153
sweet potato fries 111

Szechuan chilli dressing 42

T
tacos, chicken tinga 17
tarts: blueberry 72
  Hong Kong egg 48
  rhubarb 162
tequila: margaritas 20, 96,
  138
  tequila beyond sunrise 20
  tequila slammer 128
Thai peanut wings 132
Tintoretto 38
tofu: egg noodle, black cloud
  ear fungus & tofu salad 45
tomatoes: cherry tomato
  bruschetta 34
  Greek rice-stuffed
  tomatoes 60
  roasted tomato salsa 14
  sun-blush tomato, orange
  & burrata salad 87
  tomato bacon gratin 80
  tomato, cucumber & mint
  raita 30
tortilla, Spanish potato 54
tortilla wraps: baked tortilla
  chips 100
  chicken tinga tacos 17
  fried corn tortillas 119
  orange-braised pork
  burritos 18
truffles, Frangelico 154
tzatziki 63

V
vegetables: crispy pickled 135
  root vegetable crisps 92
  salad of roasted 171

W
waffles, cornmeal 137
walnuts: blue cheese &
  walnut bites 85
whisky: hot toddy 162
  whisky & blood orange
  cream 146
wild garlic dough balls 116
wine: chorizo in red wine 54
  sangria straight up 53

Y
yogurt dips 30, 63, 100, 124

# RECIPE CREDITS

**Valerie Aikman-Smith**
Grilled Halloumi with
Jalapeño Relish

**Brontë Aurell**
Black Rice & Salmon
Salad
Creamy Potato Salad
Dill & Apple Herring
Homemade Aquavit
Mustard Herring

**Miranda Ballard**
'Scotch Eggs'
Apple Slaw
Asparagus & Prosciutto
Gratin
Celeriac Remoulade
Chorizo & Bean Burger
Chorizo & Red Cabbage
Salad
Cured Duck & Mustard
Bruschetta
Cured Pork Kebab
Skewers
Fig Chutney
Salumi Chips
Sweet & Feisty Crème
Fraîche

**Ghillie Basan**
Little Spinach & Feta
Pastries
Mini Kebabs with
Flatbreads
Shredded Pastry Filled
with Cheese in Lemon
Syrup

**Julz Beresford**
Chorizo in Red Wine
Ham & Chicken
Croquettes

**Jordan Bourke**
Avocado Miso Dip
Choco-avo Mousse
Peach & Avocado
Panzanella

**Julia Charles**
Baked Tortilla Chips
Manchego & Olive
Pinchos
Rose & Pomegranate
Cosmo

Sangria Straight Up

**Lydia Clark**
Trio of Honey-Baked
Camembert

**Jesse Estes**
Classic Margarita
Tequila Beyond Sunrise

**Felipe Fuentes Cruz &
Ben Fordham**
Chicken Tinga Tacos
Elotes
Fried Corn Tortillas with
Chilli Tomato Sauce &
Cheese

**Ursula Ferrigno**
Herb Spelt Bread
Olive Oil & Black Pepper
Nibbles
Sardinian Pizza

**Liz Franklin**
Blue Cheese & Walnut
Bites
Negroni
Spritz
Tintoretto

**Tori Finch**
Baba Ghanoush
Rosemary Skewered
Sausages
Salad of Roasted Root
Vegetables
Scotch Quails' Eggs

**Acland Geddes**
Falafel with Tzatziki

**Laura Gladwin**
Babycakes
Pimm's Deluxe

**Victoria Glass**
Lemon Drizzle Cake

**Carole Hilker**
Avocado Margarita
Beer Margarita
Bourbon Baked Beans
Crispy Pickled Vegetables
Fried Game Hen &
Cornmeal Waffles
Homemade Cola
Homemade Lemon-Lime
Soda
Homemade Root Beer

Not Your Dad's BBQ
Wings
Spicy Grilled Orange-
Honey Mustard Wings
Thai Peanut Wings

**Jackie Kearney**
Jerusalem Artichokes

**Jenny Linford**
Cherry Tomato
Bruschetta
Fig & Honey Ricotta
Cheesecake
Flowering Chinese Chive
Prawns
Garlic & Almond
Sprouting Broccoli
Greek Rice-Stuffed
Tomatoes
Halloumi & Mushroom
Kebabs
Herbed Crushed Potatoes
Lancashire Hotpot
Leek & Potato Soup
Mushroom & Parma Ham
Pizza
Mushroom-Filled Lettuce
Cups
Patatas Bravas
Potato Pakoras
Risotto Nero with
Prawns
Sun-Blush Tomato,
Orange & Burrata
Salad
Tomato Bacon Gratin
Wild Garlic Dough Balls

**Loretta Liu**
Hong Kong Egg Tart

**Hannah Miles**
Chilli Popcorn
Salted Caramel Popcorn
Strawberry Shortcake
Layer Mousses

**Miisa Mink**
Blueberry Tart with Rye
Gradvad Lax
Rhubarb Tart

**Nitisha Patel**
Gosht Aloo Saag Masala
Naani Maa's Lemon
Pickle
Samosas
Tomato, Cucumber &
Mint Raita

**Louise Pickford**
Chicken Noodle Soup
Egg Noodle, Black Cloud
Ear Fungus & Tofu
Salad
Spring Pasta Salad Jar
Steamed Rice Noodle
Dumplings with
Scallops
Szechuan Chilli Dressing

**Ben Reed**
B-52
Hot Toddy
Perfect Manhattan
Tequila Slammer

**Annie Rigg**
Assorted Focaccia
Crostini

**Shelagh Ryan**
Chorizo, Red Pepper
& Pea Frittata
Squares
Crispy Pork Belly Bites
Lamb Koftes with Tahini
Yogurt Dip
Spiced Mixed Nuts

**Thalassa Skinner**
Apple, Sage & Calvados
Paste

**Milli Taylor**
Churros
Frangelico Truffles

**Leah Vanderveldt**
Aquafaba Pavlova
Basic Avocado Dip
Buffalo Cauliflower &
Chickpea Bowl
Creamy Chipotle Dip
Everything Avocado
Toast
Garlic Yogurt Dip

**Laura Washburn Hutton**
Artichoke, Olive &
Provolone Panini
Chilli & Lime Garlic Mayo
Classic Fries
Guacamole
Matchstick Fries
Mexican-Style Beans
Orange-Braised Pork
Burrito
Roasted Tomato Salsa
Sweet Potato Fries

# PICTURE CREDITS

**Jan Baldwin** 11b, 36, 58,
65, 92, 126, 142r, 159
**Steve Baxter** 37
Peter Cassidy
12, 16, 18, 32, 50, 53-55, 61,
66-73, 81, 86, 111, 112, 118,
119, 134b, 163
**Helen Cathcart** 56, 154
**Addie Chinn** 146
**Tara Fisher** 90, 93, 96,
98, 121
**Georgia Glynn-Smith** 63,
166, 170, 171
**Catherine Gratwicke** 38
**Louise Hagger** 48, 49
**Richard Jung** 85l, 87, 88
**Mowie Kay** 1, 4, 7-10, 39,
84, 103, 147
**Erin Kunkel** 2, 11a, 82,
142l, 164
**William Lingwood** 128,
162
**Adrian Lawrence** 169
**Alex Luck** 20, 21, 52, 64,
155, 168, 173
**Steve Painter** 74-80, 109,
110, 114, 129, 137, 140,
148, 152
**Toby Scott** 5b, 97, 101,
106, 113, 130-134a, 135,
136, 139
**Ian Wallace** 40-44, 47
**Kate Whitaker** 25, 28, 62,
85r, 122, 143, 145
**Isobel Wield** 15, 19, 172
**Clare Winfield** 3, 5a, 14,
22, 24, 26, 27, 31, 35, 46,
89, 94, 102, 105, 117, 125,
138, 144, 151, 156, 160,
161, 167

Also available from Ryland Peters & Small:

*Share* by Theo A. Michaels

*Cheese Boards to Share* by Thalassa Skinner

*Binge-Watching Eats* by Katherine Bebo